"The knowledge and unde[...]t *Your Trauma* make this one [...] f you've experienced traum[...]e part of your past, this is the [...]

—Darlene Brock, President, The Grit and Grace Project and author of *Raising Great Girls*

"Trauma is not what happens to you, but your responses to it. Caroline Beidler comes alongside as a trusted expert and gentle friend to show you how to make the changes you need to uproot those unhealthy responses and bring the light of hope to the future."

—W. Lee Warren, MD, neurosurgeon and award-winning author, and host of *The Dr. Lee Warren Podcast*

"Caroline's writing is suffused with an incredible integrity and intensity that is uplifting. Her openness, insights, and intellectual generosity make her a powerful voice in the addiction recovery literature."

—David Best, Director, Centre for Addiction Recovery Research (CARR) Leeds Trinity University

"Rife with humor, research and a poignant recounting of her and her mother's traumatic experiences, this book invites us to consider our own trauma, with Caroline providing a roadmap for how to move forward, if and when we are ready to embark on our own healing journey."

—Dawn Nickel, PhD, Founder, She Recovers Foundation

"From the first page, I was drawn into its compassionate embrace, captivated by deeply personal stories and practical wisdom that shine through like rays of hope. The love and strength guiding readers toward self-compassion and transformation could light up the world—showing us all a path to a brighter, trauma-free future."

—Mulka Nisic, Chair, Global Gender Committee, WFAD

"Caroline Beidler masterfully guides us through all the implications of what trauma does, weaving her own story throughout with superb creative writing skills. Thoroughly engaging, enlightening, and hopeful, this book is a testament to resilience and the healing power of personal narrative."

—Pastor Ed Treat, Founder and CEO, The Center of Addiction & Faith

"*You Are Not Your Trauma* is for anyone who longs for a future brighter than their past. Caroline has gifted us with a hopeful truth: healing is not a distant dream, but a tangible journey within reach. These pages offer more than just words—they offer rhythms that inspire movement toward freedom, one day at a time."

—Manda Carpenter, author of *Soul Care to Save Your Life*

"Caroline sucked me in with her personal story and beautiful, poignant writing, but her five powerful rhythms and detailed research sealed the deal that this will become a must refer book to all of my clients struggling with overcoming trauma, especially generational trauma."

—Dr. Zoe, psychotherapist, author, and speaker

"*You Are Not Your Trauma* is a compassionate guide to reclaiming your personal power and healing from traumas. Caroline and Diana offer reflection, stories and practical steps so readers can grow in resilience and grit. A must-read!"

—Susan Packard, co-founder of HGTV and author of *Fully Human*

You Are Not Your Trauma

You Are Not Your Trauma

Uproot Unhealthy Patterns, Heal the Family Tree

CAROLINE BEIDLER, MSW
with Diana Dalles, LPN, MSSW

lakedrivebooks.com

Lake Drive Books
6757 Cascade Road SE, 162
Grand Rapids, MI 49546

info@lakedrivebooks.com
lakedrivebooks.com
@lakedrivebooks

Publishing books that help you heal, grow, and discover.

Paperback ISBN: 978-1-957687-53-7
E-book ISBN: 978-1-957687-54-4

Library of Congress Control Number: 2024910969

Cover design by Laura Duffy
Cover illustration by Maljuk/iStock
Author photographs by Martha Howell and Nicholas Laufenberg

For my mother: thank you for choosing to heal.

To my dear daughter: because you've shared your story, you've inspired me to be vulnerable and share mine.

CONTENTS

*God is making miracles to free us from
the shame that haunts us.*

—Cole Arthur Riley

Introduction
Ripe with Possibility

When I found out I was pregnant, I had to sit down.

The chair I fell into was a reupholstered antique that had once belonged to my great-grandmother. I never knew much about her other than her husband was a farmer who looked (in the one picture I saw of him) like Ryan Gosling in *The Notebook*, only with real farmer biceps—the kind of muscles that pull soldiers up out of foxholes.

I stared at the pregnancy stick my work friend said I should drive to Walgreens to buy because that's what women do when they miss their period. I grabbed onto the smooth wooden arms of the chair, the arms that my ancestor had rested her own hands on. I looked down at the rough, gold material that was selected to cover over the coils and puffs of whatever is on the inside of these old chairs.

I didn't think this was something I'd ever do—buy a pregnancy test. I had been married for only six weeks. I didn't think I could even have children. I'd had enough unsafe sex to have birthed a football team by then. But I took the test (because that's what women do, my friend said). And I waited there for almost an hour with a towel covering the little window of results.

Despite things being pretty amazing by this point in my life and recovery, considering all the trauma, brokenness, and years of unhealthy patterns I'd lived through, I still tiptoed around life. Even though, six weeks before, I had walked down the aisle to Neil Diamond's "Sweet Caroline," surprising the heck out of my family. Even though they all sang along as I smiled through tears of joy and looked toward a stable, handsome, driven, and smart green-eyed man.*

Somewhere inside, I still harbored the secret thought that God was going to disappoint me. That *I* was going to disappoint me. I'd be able to yell, "See! I knew I couldn't trust you!"

"See, your trauma is too much."

"*You* are too much."

Our early October wedding was a dream, with the kind of wind that kicks up Lake Michigan in a beautiful frenzy. A dusting of yellow leaves and fading hydrangeas adorned the ceremony of only a few close family and friends. I wore a dress that was way puffier than I had envisioned. My longing for something sleek and classy and crème flew out the window as soon as I tried on this once-in-a-lifetime gown that made me feel like a combination between Xena the Warrior Princess and a giant tulle cupcake.

We picked out the flowers the morning of the ceremony at a small floral shop where the owner looked on, disgusted

---

* As a sidenote: It's okay to keep our prayers specific when we are praying for a mate or partner. My prayer was a tall, green-eyed, supersmart hunk of a man who challenged me intellectually and spiritually, and that is exactly what I got. He's a theoretical physicist and Methodist. Go figure.

(apparently wedding parties picking out flowers in the morning for that afternoon's wedding is looked down upon). My best person and I made our bouquets on the gray-marbled kitchen counter of an Airbnb right before driving to the old white farmhouse where the hunky physicist and I said our vows under the most glorious tree I'd ever seen, with gray branches reaching toward the heavens.

I was the happiest warrior cupcake ever.

But even as it was happening in real time, I couldn't believe that it was happening for me (*it* meaning a "normal life").

Just like the moment I sat on the edge of the gold chair that had so lovingly cradled my ancestors' butts and stared at the stick I had just peed on. I kept shaking my head no. I kept looking at it and then reading the instructions again.

One line – not pregnant.

Two lines = pregnant.

Do I have one line or two?

I looked down.

Two.

Wait.

Is that . . . ?

(Reading the box again.)

One line – not pregnant.

Two lines = pregnant.

TWO?!

Once it finally sank in, I jumped up and sat down, then walked around as if in a trance—an "I can't believe I am pregnant! Am I pregnant?!" stupor. I smiled the half smile of someone who wasn't quite sure if I should be happy. *Is this going to last?* The fear already creeping in.

But I *was*—I was ridiculously happy. I couldn't believe it. I couldn't believe that I actually got pregnant. I had always had an inkling that if I was able to have kids, I would have had them by then—out of wedlock, as I so bluntly alluded to earlier. Plus, I'd had my share of sexually transmitted infections that can impact a woman's ability to conceive, or so Google informed me.

I praised God.

I cried.

I praised God again.

A snippet of a quote from one of my favorite authors, Brennan Manning, came to mind: "Freedom brings an appreciation for the lessons of captivity."[1]

Then I wondered what the hell I was going to do.

My husband was away on a work trip in San Diego doing some important sciencey stuff that I still can't explain. He wouldn't be home until around midnight when I was supposed to meet him at the airport. So, I decided to do what many women do when we find out we're pregnant: I went shopping.

I strolled the baby aisle and brushed my fingers against soft muslin and plush blankets and the teeniest, tiniest onesies and miniature gloves and hats and little slippers with the heads and ears of forest creatures like bunnies and foxes and bears. Around me were other women who looked like me. Some were either starry-eyed with tight tummies or a little more drained-looking with basketballs in their shirts. Then there were the women I couldn't yet make eye contact with who looked like someone had sucked their insides out with a straw, with one baby tugging a breast, another in a stroller, and one pulled along by the armpit.

It was winter, just before Christmas, so I found the most adorable tiny faux leather boots with off-white fluff coming out the top. Both shoes fit on one of my open hands. I stared at these tiny shoes. There was going to be a little human in these shoes (I did not know yet that there were going to be two little humans). I searched the clothing and tried to find something gender neutral. Not too frilly. I found a forest green and navy long-sleeved onesie that said something about going on a journey.

This moment was like coming out of a strange wilderness. God showed up again. Despite my fear and unbelief. Despite my doubt that good things were going to keep happening, God showed up in a heart-wrenchingly beautiful way: I was pregnant. I couldn't stop saying it.

On the way home from picking Matt up at the airport, I was so nervous I could barely breathe in the car. I had to roll the window down, and the night air wafted in.

Deep breaths.

You can do this.

I didn't exactly know what I was going to do. How was I going to say it? When should I tell him? We drove the familiar path back to our small rented house. Matt talked about his work, but I could tell he was tired from being on a plane for hours, still adjusting to having feet on the ground.

We arrived and the dogs greeted us. Matt set his bag down and went to the bathroom.

This was my chance. Even though he was exhausted and I was unsure, I decided I had to tell him. Immediately. I took out the little boots and set them against the wall near the front door where the rest of our shoes were lined up.

I smiled. This was *really* happening.

When he came upstairs, I led him to the doorway and pointed. I couldn't even say the words.

He looked at me in shock.

That was the beginning of everything.

At that moment, I realized that *we can be part of a new story.* We are not our trauma.

———

Olive trees stand apart from each other like distant lovers. The thick trunks lead into a chaotic crisscross of limbs and grayish-brown question marks. It isn't a blissful picture with angelic clouds and a rainbow of flowers. Instead, a grove of olives is straight out of a scene from *Lord of the Rings* when you know everything is about ready to go to hell.

Mature olive trees are eerily beautiful though. In all their mangledness, there is something about them: Strength? Life? Hope?

What appears from the tips of the most distorted branches is a verdancy that surprises: a flutter of grassy green and a glint of yellow in the light, like a clapping Colorado aspen.

Russell Stafford is a self-proclaimed "hortiholic and plant evangelist" and wrote an article called "Specimen Trees and Shrubs with Elegantly Twisted Branches." In it, he talks about a number of trees, like the olive, that are zigged and zagged from the main trunk.

Stafford writes, "Some trees are just twisted—literally. Rather than growing in the usual linear pattern, their stems crazily zig and zag, each segment veering in a different direction from the previous one."[2]

He goes on to talk about a variety of crooked trees like the scarlet curls willow, contorted beech, and dragon's claw willow. They each have branches that twist and curl and do backflips into the sky. They are characterized by "whimsically erratic angles" and "theatrically wild silhouettes," according to Stafford. There is less pattern and regularity. No predictability. Yet something about them makes them stand out. Makes you stare. Wonder.

They are lovely.

Hardy.

Add variance to the landscape.

These trees, like the olive, make you stop and think and (for people like me) wonder at the God who created such variety. Such beauty from the misshapen.

My own life has been like this: a branch from a family tree that is as bent and meandering as a dragon mulberry. I have wandered into painful scenes, my own personal Garden of Gethsemane, surrounded by a family that is less than perfect. Family that is twisted. Struggling. Absent. I, too, have asked questions in this garden and struggled my way to recover from trauma: death, divorce, addiction, and sexual violence. I asked God, "If you are really here, why do you allow such things?"

Let this cup pass from me.

I have asked aloud, "Where is God when it hurts?" And I have wondered in secret why some families are sturdy like oak trees and mine is slow to grow and low to the ground.* Yet I've also experienced the other side of the questions. Where the light hits just so and dances on the forest floor. Where a garden of questions is transformed into a prairie of peace. The place where I know God has a plan and a purpose. And the plan and purpose are good.

Thy will be done.

---

* *Where Is God When It Hurts?* is one of my favorite books by Philip Yancey.

As a now East Tennessean, I've looked out my window at the towering ash and cedar trees around us and marveled at their strength. How when the wind sweeps through the mountain ridges, only the tops of the branches sway. Roots twisted below, stretching in and out among the rock, they get water and nutrient-rich soil wherever they can. Making it against all odds. Born to be resilient. Created for recovery.

The journey we are about to go on together is an exploration into the concept of intergenerational or family trauma and how it can nestle into the branches of our family trees without our even being aware of it. This book is also a journey of recovery through trauma and its symptoms and unhealthy patterns that mirror my mother's story with uncanny particularity (you'll see why in a bit).

Dr. Bessel van der Kolk, the preeminent researcher on trauma, says that regardless of the specifics, most of us are survivors of trauma in some form. Most of us, to live healthy lives and make healthy choices, need to learn how to "develop a mind that heals."[3] We must learn how to have compassion for our stories.

Even if the specifics of our stories are different, we can relate to one another. Even if your idea of recovery is different from mine, we no doubt have something in our pasts or in our families' pasts that keeps us from living the lives we dream of. My mother and I invite you into our stories so that you can see yours, perhaps, in a new way.

Over time, I've come to believe that we can gain the ability to see our stories and our experiences with new eyes. By searching the past for clues, we can discover how the muck of our own lives resembles, in some ways, that of our mothers, grandmothers, great-grandmothers, or other family members.

And importantly, we can learn that we don't have to stay stuck there. We can move into a place where we feel safe in our own bodies, where we can hold our stories with compassion and hope. We can choose healing today for our children's tomorrow. We don't have to identify with our trauma any longer.

I've also uncovered, along a recovery journey, that we should ask these questions: What is it about our family trees that allows particular forms of trauma to spread like a disease? Why do some of our lineages foster hardships like sexual trauma, addiction, unhealthy relationships, and more? And how can we move beyond a cycle of family brokenness, suffering, and trauma? This allows us to open our hearts and minds to learn and see new things about our experience.

I love the way Trey Ferguson in *Theologizin' Bigger* puts it:

> We are shaped by our experiences. We carry many of the lessons we come across—even some of the ones we'd rather leave behind. We are marked by our trauma. Our communities and families of origin have left their fingerprints at the core of our being.[4]

While we may be marked by our trauma, we can live in freedom, breaking the cycle. We can live more joyfully and ensure that our children don't have to live in our chains. We can heal the tree and experience the spaciousness of a new identity.

In this book, I'm going to share with you what I've learned about intergenerational trauma and recovery from my personal experience, from research, and from your stories. Together, we are also going to uncover that healing is deeper than a trending TED Talks big idea. Recovery is deeper than a formula designed to concoct the right solution. Recovery isn't a moment in time where we arrive. Recovery is a *process*. And we owe it to the next generation to go deeper with our healing.

I identify as a woman in recovery (from addiction, trauma, anxiety, depression, men, ice cream, the list goes on) and also an expert in the field of behavioral health and social work, having worked with thousands of individuals looking for solutions. I've also had the opportunity to build things like nonprofit recovery homes for women, statewide peer support organizations, and even a recovery ministry, all centered on one truth: transformation is possible. Our stories, even the broken pieces, can be redeemed.

I know this. People I've worked with have experienced it. I've witnessed the way recovery brings light back to the eyes. Maybe you have too.

I'm also a Christian. I know—please don't hold this against me. Some of you may be challenged by this.

Saying such a thing is weighty in our culture today. It may even carry uncomfortable weight in your own life because of religious trauma. I feel you and I've been there. I include parts of my spiritual path along our journey together because that is a large part of my story. I say all of this because I don't want you to choke on your chai when, along with evidence-based information, I include some references from scripture or other recovery-related texts that also help with transformation. My encouragement to you is to keep reading. Will you consider the multiple pathways we may find along the road to healing?

In this book, for all my list-lovers out there, I also outline a series of five rhythms that help guide us to a greater understanding and acceptance of our past and toward a freer recovery. They can be transformational focus points. This framework can lead us to break free from past wounds or work to disrupt them.

This is a bold statement and a weighty promise, I know, but I truly believe these rhythms can help your life the way they have helped—and continue to help—mine.

The five rhythms are:

Protect the Temple—Honoring the Self
Practice Forgiveness—Radical Compassion
Lean In to the Struggle—Everyday Courage
Get Real—Soul Honesty
Let God—Living Open-Handed

These rhythms are grounded in the truth that's been woven across time and curls through the earth like the roots of an old oak. Healing can happen. No matter the weight of our past and no matter our monsters or the specifics of our trauma. The future is ripe with possibility. Transformation is possible.

Again, these steps aren't a gimmicky formula. For you, sweet reader, these rhythms create *movement*. They will help you inch toward freedom one day at a time. Progress over perfection. Throughout the stories in this book, I hope that you are able to feel this movement in your own story.

It's tough to understand why trauma exists. Over the years, I've had (and heard) so many questions like: Why do we have to experience suffering at all? How can we find purpose in the pain? What do we do with what we find?

I love what Joan Walsh Anglund, a children's book author, wrote in a poetry collection entitled *A Cup of Sun*: "A bird doesn't sing because it has an answer, it sings because it has a song."[5]

We say in addiction recovery that our "experience, strength, and hope" can help another alcoholic or addict. I love this. It reminds me that I may not have all the answers about why there is so much hurt and trouble in the world, or why you experienced what you did (or are experiencing now), but I do know that stories can bring healing. From a tiny seed can sprout magnificent trees that bear fruit.

It's a glorious and juicy thought. Whether it's shared around a circle of chairs in AA, NA, or another type of support group, told on the phone with a friend we trust, or found in the pages of this book. We don't have the privilege of keeping our healing to ourselves.

To help us understand how intergenerational trauma can affect us today, I've included excerpts from my mother's journal in this book. They appear as short interludes along the way. These excerpts, written by her hand, will not only shed light on my story but demonstrate the insidious nature of trauma and why we must work to disrupt it. It is an honor to include part of my mother's story in this book. I'm so grateful for her experience, strength, hope, and courage.

Finally, as a disclaimer, I'd like to add that my journey is not finished. What I preach, I practice (on good days) or strive to do (on rough ones). Though I write about rhythms, I'm not always living in them. I admit that readily because I know that in weakness lies my strength and the truth that God can do for me what I cannot do for or by myself.*,[6] Together, we are on this journey toward healing and wholeness. Let's get to it.

---

* This alludes to the twelfth promise in the AA Big Book: "We will suddenly realize that God is doing for us what we could not do for ourselves."

Rhythm 1

Protect the Temple—Honoring the Self

Chapter 1

Growing Through It

Janie saw her life like a great tree in leaf with the things suffered, things enjoyed, things done and undone. Dawn and doom was in the branches.
—Zora Neale Hurston, *Their Eyes Were Watching God*

I grabbed my bag and left the building, then frantically searched for my cell phone. Gum, tampons, crumpled receipts like confetti. A quick scroll through my recent calls list and I found her.

"Mom?"

She answered the other line like she usually did, with a mother's prophetic ear, knowing immediately that something was off.

"Are you okay?"

"No."

It wasn't until I had several years of sobriety that I realized how much help I really needed. I was in graduate school, going back to become a mental health counselor (or so I thought at the time; God had other plans). I knew that I wanted to help other women who had lived through what I did, so I thought this was the best route to go. For the graduate program, we had to pick an internship. An adviser helped me select one that was very much outside my comfort zone but that he thought would fit me well as a "nontraditional" student (he could have just said "old").

My internship was with an addiction treatment center for veterans at a local VA hospital, near where I lived at the time. I have a long history of military service in my family and also personal history with trauma and PTSD, so this placement fit on a number of levels.

What I didn't realize when I signed up, but quickly learned while working with veterans and their challenges, was how triggering it would be for me as a sexual violence survivor. I didn't have the language at the time to express what I was experiencing—flashbacks, dissociation, flat affect, and shutting down—but it hit me like a freight train. The trauma from my past was different from many of the veterans in the treatment center, but the effects were the same. I started seeing a therapist again once I realized how bad the anxiety and related trauma symptoms were getting. Though I had never been in combat, it felt like I was entering a war zone.

During this time, I was learning how to conduct group therapy and at the same time feeling like I was going through the treatment myself. During one particular group, the room started to spin and a familiar choking feeling settled in the back of my throat. Beads of sweat formed on my forehead, and I looked down at my shaking hands in my lap. All I could smell was the hollow antiseptic that anyone who has been to addiction treatment knows about. I ran from the room and almost vomited in the group facilitator's office.

How could I share all of this with my mother? I didn't know where to start.

I sat in silence on the other end of the line as I walked my dog around the little inlet by my rented house. A man rode by on his bike with a leather bag and reflective shoes. A woman walked by with her black lab that pulled on his leash the way an old dog does: with feigned vigor—then on to the next smell.

"I don't know, Mom. It's something about all those men. The group room. Walls closing in. I'm having flashbacks again, but the memories are fuzzy. Like bad cell reception."

She was quiet.

I hesitated to bring anything up to her because of her own struggles. I wasn't the only one to experience trauma, including sexual violence. We had more in common than just the way we said "Oh, gosh!" like northerners. There were other experiences buried beneath the surface. Like roots intertwined below ground.

I could hear her take a long, slow breath.

"Your body remembers?"

"Exactly."

At a Crossroads

A couple days before this call with my mother, I sat stopped at a red light on my road bike, watching the whale-sized buses zoom past. It frightened me where my mind went.

I didn't ride my bike in front of the moving bus, but at the time, I recall feeling like it wasn't out of the realm of possibility. What started happening in my body and mind—in early recovery—caught me off guard. Instead of protecting the temple of my personhood, I felt pulled toward ending it. The pain was so great.

The pain, instead of being buried deep inside, was starting to resurface, taking shape. I could finally look at the pain and say, "There it is!" I was learning for the first time in my life how fully entrenched trauma and its symptoms were in my mind and body, and how, if I wanted to grow in my addiction recovery or even stay in abstinence-based recovery, I was going to need to do something about it. It was time.

I'm not the only one. According to the National Institute on Drug Abuse, nearly 80 percent of women have experienced some type of trauma.[7] Research also shows how, along with the interconnection of trauma and addiction, there is an increased risk for developing PTSD for those who have experienced trauma, particularly those who have experienced sexual trauma.[8]

What does this mean? Many women—I'd argue most women—have trauma that we need to address to grow and move forward in life and recovery. Many of our temples, our bodies, have been hurt. It is under the surface, bubbling up with certain symptoms, unhealthy patterns, or behaviors, but it's very real. Trauma, including family trauma, is affecting our lives more than we often recognize.

What are some of the ways that past trauma has resurfaced in your life or is resurfacing as we have this conversation together? Are there things from your own life or your parents' lives (or their parents' lives) that are creeping into your every day and preventing you from living in freedom? What is disrupting your peace or preventing you from honoring your self and story?

Maybe you are like me and my mother and lived through sexual violence or abuse. Maybe you are a military veteran and have had to witness things and do the things of nightmares. Maybe yours is a religious trauma that impacts the way you connect with God, the church, or anyone who claims to be a part of a family of faith. Divorce, neglect, natural disaster, poverty, racism, colonialism, the patriarchy (as my fellow feminist friends say). There are as many shades of trauma and hurt as there are pathways of recovery. There are so many ways that our temples are desecrated.

The good news is that we don't have to live chained to those things that haunt our family trees. We are called to love each other and, just as importantly, to love ourselves and honor our lives. But how can we do this when we might be weighed down by trauma?

We Aren't Crazy

It took me too long to get to a place where healing could begin. Or, perhaps a better way to say this is that it took me too long to be open to healing. Can you relate? Dealing with my traumatic history was something I continued to run from for years. This impacted so much of my actions throughout life and also how I viewed, valued, and dishonored myself.

When I was in active addiction, I was plagued by thoughts and questions like: "Why do I need to use to feel normal or calm?" "Why am I so out of control?" "What's wrong with me?" I used the stigmatizing and hurtful word "crazy" to describe myself and my actions.

Even in sobriety, I often wondered, "If I am alcohol- and drug-free, why am I still hurting so much?"

I thought that ending the addiction (or at least stalling it) was enough. The flashbacks, nightmares, anxiety, depression, lingering toxic stress, trust issues, relationship disasters, boundary issues, disordered eating, and trouble sleeping—I thought that somehow it was all going to magically disappear after I quit drinking and drugging.

It didn't.

The first part of moving toward healing that we are exploring together is the concept of protecting the temple and honoring the self. Importantly, to do this, we need to learn more about ourselves. It might be painful, and it definitely won't be comfortable, but when we can look at our past and examine how family or intergenerational trauma might be impacting our lives today, we can learn more about why protecting the temple and honoring ourselves is important.

You may not identify with being in addiction recovery, and that's okay. Maybe drinking and drugging isn't your thing. Maybe it's more like shopping or binge-watching or having lots of sex (or even sexual fantasies). Humans are a creative species. We've come up with a whole array of options to escape and numb the pain of what we've experienced. There are about as many ways to become numb as there are cowboy dramas with hunks on horsebacks.

I believe that recovery is for everyone, and we are all in recovery from something.

Did you know that during a traumatic event, the body and mind tries to protect itself? The body and brain shut down all nonessential processes and get stuck in survival mode. This is when the sympathetic nervous system increases stress hormones and prepares the body to fight, flee, or freeze. Trauma propels the body and nervous system into a state that causes us to be unable to self-regulate. In other words, we are in overdrive.

Not surprisingly, our systems get all sorts of messed up. Our nervous systems get stuck in the "on" position and lead us to be overstimulated, unable to calm, and always in a state of "fight or flight" or near it. Or, if not this, feeling numb, detached, or dissociated. Maybe you are feeling this now as you read this. If so, I want to remind you that there is a tool I've included at the end of the book that offers a set of exercises that you can try if you are feeling triggered. I also want to encourage you to seek outside support if you need it—or if you feel moved toward deeper exploration into these topics. Seeking therapy, counseling, and other resources can help guide you into greater freedom and healing too, and this book should not replace those in-person supports.*

Dr. Bessel van der Kolk, along with being a famous trauma researcher, also wrote a foundational book called *The Body Keeps the Score*. He asserts that "as long as the trauma is not resolved, the stress hormones that the body secretes to protect itself keep circulating, and the defensive movements and emotional responses keep getting replayed."[9] It's no wonder that so many of us turn to unhealthy coping mechanisms to ease this suffering in our bodies, minds, and spirits, one of the most popular being substances like alcohol and other drugs.

Regardless of what comes first, the unhealthy coping or the trauma, like the chicken or the egg argument, we need to start talking about it. What happened, how we feel today, and importantly, how its lineage creeps up our family tree like the emerald ash borer.[†] When we start to recognize the patterns, we can start to rebuild.

---

* If you are wondering, I still see a therapist when I need to dive deeper into issues as a way to protect and honor myself. Hey, Lindsey!

[†] The emerald ash borer is a beetle that is native to northeastern Asia that feeds on ash trees, devouring forests and neighborhoods of this waning species of tree. We've had to have several of these trees cut down in our yard in East Tennessee because they've been infected.

Healing is not a mystery. It's not reserved for the ultrareligious or perfect AA member or lifelong counselee. Healing can be a choice. Each day is an opportunity to choose to do the next right thing. To show up. To feel. Sometimes, this next right thing is choosing to embrace all of our story, including the painful parts we'd rather keep buried. Not to grip them too tightly but to learn and grow beyond them so we can be fully present for the next amazing chapter. Sometimes, the next right thing is being open to a movement of God, a cleaning out, a starting again. A disruption.

Etched in Stone?

Trauma can feel final. Like what happens to us is etched in stone, forever visible even when faded, like indigenous cave dwelling art. Each stroke is like an old riverbed, telling secrets of the past. I remember feeling this way after years of instability in the wake of my parents' divorce. My mother left when my brother and I were still in diapers. Our lives were measured by every other weekends when we saw her, unable to understand more of the *why* until years, decades later. Only seeing the surface of things: She wasn't happy. She felt like she had to leave. The truth buried deep in the earth. Not knowing that the things that happen to us and to our families can become a part of us, a part of our genetic makeup, and breathe into our very lives today. This is what researchers today call epigenetics.

Epigenetics is the study of how your behaviors and environment can cause changes that affect the way your genes work, according to the National Institute of Health.[10] Your family's pattern of physical, sexual, or emotional abuse. The way you only feel worth when you are worshipping at the temple of business or money, or the way you obsess over your body image. When we look into the mirror, our souls may see our ancestors' transgressions—alive and breathing in our minds and bodies. But sometimes—and quite often—we don't recognize this. We don't recognize the impact of previous generations on our current lives.

So how can we honor the self when we feel trapped in a cycle of unhealthy patterns like our family members? How can we embrace healing when doubt creeps in and it's tough to imagine ever living free of whatever might consume us?

On the outside, it might appear hopeless that we should ever heal or become new branches, ones that come from the old roots of human brokenness and ugliness and trauma. It feels hopeless that we might ever set our monsters down. And indeed, it is hopeless . . . *Until*.

You see, there is a sweet place in all this mess where God comes in. Ever since time began and the first candle star was lit in the sky. Ever since God's prophet Isaiah uttered the visionary words, "Out of the stump of David's family will grow a shoot— yes, a new Branch bearing fruit from the old root" (Isaiah 11:1, Life Recovery Bible, NLT).

Out of all our family trees something incredible can grow: new branches that bear fruit.

Have you ever seen a shoot growing up out of an old stump that's been cut down? A fresh, new, young green thing that's reaching toward the light? It's a beautiful sight. A picture of hope. If you don't yet believe that things can get better—that you can be this fresh, new, young, green thing—hold on. We will get there together.

Chapter 2

Heavy Monsters

Freedom from strongholds is serious business.

—Beth Moore

In her memoir *Wild*, Cheryl Strayed talks about lugging around a fifty-pound pack that she named Monster. When Cheryl first started out hiking the Pacific Crest Trail after a divorce and addiction to heroin, Monster was a behemoth, something she could barely pick up and strap to her skinny shoulders. Cheryl writes:

> Standing, it came up to my waist. I gripped it and bent to lift it.
>
> It wouldn't budge.
>
> I squatted and grasped its frame more robustly and tried to lift it again. Again, it did not move. Not even an inch. I tried to lift it with both hands, with my legs braced beneath me, while attempting to wrap it in a bear hug, with all of my breath and my might and my will, with everything in me. And still it would not come.

It was exactly like attempting to lift a Volkswagen Beetle. It looked so cute, so *ready* to be lifted—and yet, it was impossible.[11]

Monster carried around all sorts of odds and ends and necessities and frivolities. Monster liked to read at night (even in the wilderness) and so toted heavy books, along with extra clothes and ice picks and even a string of condoms. Monster liked to remind Cheryl of her frailty and brokenness, dig into her skin, and make raw the points where friction happened. Little did Monster know, most of what it carried wouldn't be needed out there on the trail. Monster needed a nice man on his own hike on the PCT to stop and help it go through items one by one to whittle down the weight.

Eventually, Cheryl and Monster became friends. After all, it was Monster that made it possible for her to go on a solo thousand-mile journey on the PCT without getting mauled by bears or a couple of drunk hillbillies. Monster kept what Cheryl needed, though she may not have always recognized she needed it. Monster also encouraged her to let go of the things she no longer needed to carry.

What is the baggage that is preventing you from honoring yourself and protecting the lovely temple that is you? Maybe it's something that happened when you were a kid that you haven't told anyone about. Maybe it's that one thing you did that one time. Maybe it is *all the things* that weigh you down so much that you feel like you must pick up that bottle of wine or prescription or vape pen or pint of ice cream on the way home from the pickup line outside your kids' school or work.

Worst-Case Scenario Survivors

I once texted my friend and let her know some really good news. It was the kind of news that you have to tell all the people you love—right that second. It's too good to keep to yourself. I love the this-is-so-good-I-just-have-to-tell-you messages. Well, she still hasn't gotten back to me. My bestie.

I'm sure she has a good reason. Perhaps she missed it. Perhaps she saw it first thing in the morning, then got distracted. Perhaps she actually did type back and then forgot to send. Or maybe she just doesn't care. But it really doesn't matter the reason. If I am in a not-so-great place ("spiritually unfit" as another friend in recovery likes to say), I will whip this up into a frenzy of self-loathing in my mind. With one missed text, I am:

Silly.

Foolish.

Insecure.

Unimportant.

Unloved.

Then to top it all off, I notice that a weight begins to form on my shoulders, pressing me down,

down,

down,

making every step the tiniest bit more uncomfortable,

draining,

painful,

excruciating.

Monster is back. The biggest, heaviest piece of baggage you can imagine.

It's not just my friend (though I have enough trust issues for an anthology); this can happen in any situation. Text. Email.

Talks with my hubby. Tea with the church ladies. After speaking at an event. Or even *while* I am speaking. (Don't these people know what a freak and fraud I am?) Standing in a cloud of vape smoke outside a recovery meeting. Singing self-consciously in the sanctuary. If I am not careful, I start to believe some pretty insidious lies about myself. Again.

That's the thing about Monster. He knows how and where to weigh me down.

My past is not pitch-perfect. It's dirty. Like the TV series *Shameless*, which is about a family with their own baggage, their own monsters. You don't like it, but you can't look away. It's filled with the furthest things from "Christian" and at the same time, so much of what Jesus came to conquer. Addiction, sexual immorality, violence, trauma, mental illness, the list goes on and gets more and more like an X-rated after-school special.

I am also a worst-case scenario survivor. Perhaps you can relate?

Even though I am healed from so much of the dark and shameful parts of my past, the mess, the heavy stuff I've carried for years, can come seeping back in without my even being aware of it. My temple, my body, remembers and carries these things with me.

Maybe you have those things that bring Monster back too.

Maybe you are already on a trauma healing journey or have been for years and are wanting more—yet still struggle with flashbacks and dissociation and unhealthy relationships (I'll get to more of what trauma symptoms look like soon).

I recently heard of a good friend in recovery going back out (otherwise known as "relapsing" or a "recurrence of use") after a series of good stresses brought back flashes of the old stress.

Something triggered them in her soul. Something hidden, yet still there. And she picked the bottle back up after years of living free from substances.

Monster waits too.

When We Feel Bad about Good Things

The other night I actually had to google this exact phrase: "Why do I feel bad when good things happen?"

And you know what? Amazingly (or not), Google had an answer for me in the form of someone else's thoughts in a blog post: the reason why I have a hard time when good things happen is because of my past.

It's Monster's fault.

In the past, when good things happened, they were usually followed by bad things or negative reactions or responses or no responses, so my brain learned that over time, when good things happen, they can't be trusted. If you are a trauma survivor too, you know what I'm talking about.

Some people call it "waiting for the other shoe to drop." Those of us who experience it know that a more accurate way to phrase it is this: "When the sky falls in on itself and the earth swallows it and then belches molten lava."

I'll give you some examples.

As my wedding day approached, I imagined a far-fetched scenario where my now-husband was in a horrific shipwreck. (Note: he never travels by boat.) When I found out I was pregnant, I was sure it wasn't going to last. When I found out I landed a publisher for my first book, *Downstairs Church*, my stomach twisted in sailor knots, I felt dizzy and hot and started dissociating. For those of you who don't have PTSD, this is when you feel like you are outside your body looking in. It's a strange, otherworldly experience that feels like eating a McDonald's hamburger with psychedelic mushrooms stuffed inside (according to a friend) or like being in a bubble where everything on the outside looks a little grainy, like a photo taken with one of the first cell phones.

So it's not surprising that our default at times (even after years of work and healing) is not to trust the good. It's not to run at it with open arms and an open heart with a cheesy, joyful grin or to do one of those weird synchronized dance moves on TikTok. It's to quickly run and hide, get as far away from the good stuff as possible, because if we can protect ourselves from it, it won't be able to hurt us first. If we expect the worst, then when the good stuff does happen, we can't believe it—even if we see it with our own eyes.

Trauma manifests in all sorts of gnarly ways like this: always waiting for something bad to happen.

Emotional and psychological symptoms can include:

- Confusion, difficulty concentrating
- Anger, irritability, mood swings
- Anxiety and fear
- Guilt, shame, self-blame
- Withdrawing from others
- Feeling sad or hopeless
- Feeling disconnected or numb

Physical symptoms that plague us might be:

- Insomnia or nightmares
- Fatigue

- Being startled easily
- Difficulty concentrating
- Racing heartbeat
- Edginess and agitation
- Aches and pains
- Muscle tension
- Being unable to express affection
- Doing things that could be self-destructive or reckless
- Using alcohol or drugs to avoid memories

That's a pretty intense list. Trauma can affect you physically, emotionally, and spiritually. You may be able to relate with being overwhelmed by anxiety, anger, restlessness, panic, and hyperactivity. These are symptoms that can all be present after being triggered by a traumatic event. Even years later. Generations later.

The Diary of Us

Doe-eyed Anne Frank wrote in her famous autobiography *The Diary of a Young Girl*, "I think a lot, but I don't say much."[12] Little did she know she would end up saying more about the period of time she lived through—the Holocaust—than almost anyone else. School children all over the world have read her book and learned about the events that led to the horrific killings of approximately six million people, including Anne.

When I read her diary as a child, her words echoed in my heart, a reminder that I was not the only young girl to experience tragedy. Even though I have never lived through the severe pain and tragedy in the magnitude that she did, her words connected with my soul's primal sound: the language of suffering.

The smile on her face in most of the pictures that remain of her are forever imprinted in my mind where I keep things that both startle and shake me awake.

In the 1960s, a Canadian psychiatrist by the name of Dr. Vivian M. Rakoff started noticing something among children of Holocaust survivors: the rates of emotional struggle and psychological distress were off the charts.[13] Somehow what their ancestors had lived through—the night raids and internment camps and smell of burning flesh—became a part of their own experience. This was the moment that the concept of intergenerational trauma was born. Or as Clarice Wilsey, a daughter of a WWII soldier, said, "This is when the Dachau demons entered our living room."

Intergenerational trauma is a concept used to describe how the traumatic effects of a historical event are transmitted from one generation to the next. This transmission can manifest in a variety of ways, from unhealthy coping skills to emotional abuse or neglect, and even replaying the cause of trauma, as is sometimes the case for survivors of sexual violence.

Another generation after this, for the children's children of Holocaust survivors, more research was conducted that showed how grandchildren of Holocaust survivors were referred for mental health care 300 percent more than the general population.[14] Dr. Gayani DeSilva, a child and adolescent psychologist, notes, "Trauma affects genetic processes, leading to traumatic reactivity being heightened in populations who experience a great deal of trauma."[15] A simpler way to put it? Trauma causes havoc on our minds, bodies, and spirits, and this can impact our families for generations to come.

This is not just a convenient hypothesis from someone whose family lineage has been rocked to the core with trauma in varying shades of sludge. Research shows intergenerational trauma is the story of our lives, written in our family diaries. People's experiences of surviving horrible trauma like war and slavery have led to correlations that are too strong to dismiss.

Our own stories point to the truth too.

Yet we are silent. Despite trauma's prevalence, we rarely talk about how past events in the lives of our parents and grandparents affect us today, much less know about the concept of generational trauma or even trauma itself. We seldom acknowledge it in our family conversations, and almost never in recovery spaces. And in faith spaces? You tell me. It's part of why I wanted to share this book with you.

We don't talk about how our family's past is connected to our own. That what happened to our predecessors in yellow-tinted, black-and-white photos with stoic faces still affects (or can affect) our and our children's everyday lives. The weight set down by one generation can be picked up by another.

And yet, it doesn't have to be like this.

Just because we are living in the shadow of our past trauma and experiencing its aftershocks today, doesn't mean we have to stay there. We can crawl out of the rubble together and learn how to love ourselves. We can build healthy coping strategies and boundaries that will move us toward healing and self-love. Not the selfish kind of self-love, but the necessary kind.

———

What happened to my family—to my mother and me? At this point in the book, you might be asking yourself this question, and for good reason.

My mother and I (along with other family members) discussed this at length. What to include, what not to include. What
to share and how to share it. If you can believe it or not, there
have been whole sections of this book missing, having never
even been written, because that's how much sensitivity is needed
in the retelling of trauma that is not your own to fully tell.

After much discussion, especially with my mother, we
came to a place together that has purpose and feels right.

Ultimately the answer to the questions you might be having is this:

Have members of my family experienced things like
trauma from war, poverty, sexual abuse, emotional neglect,
misogyny, and more?

Yes.

Are there unknowns that course through the veins of my
family tree that I'll never know, asking the same questions you
might be asking now?

Who?

What?

When?

How?

Yes.

The specifics of our trauma, while we may share details
here and there like flitting leaves in fall, is not what this book is
about.

Trauma happens to all of us in varying degrees, because we
are human. It is in our humanness and shared experience,
regardless of the particulars, that we can connect.

This book is about you, sweet reader, and about those
things that you've experienced that you long to rise above. You

may ache for more. More detail. More grit. You may want to know *why*—we are human after all and like to experience the world in context.

But why isn't as important as *how*.

Regardless of the specifics, how can we move toward healing together?

You might be able to fit the inklings together as you read pieces of my mother's story in her own words and pieces of my own, or you may be left wondering. My encouragement to you in your questioning is this: regardless of the particulars of our stories, *how* does this connect to your own story?

Chapter 3

Looking for Love

Only after disaster can we be resurrected. It's only after you've lost everything that you're free to do anything. Nothing is static, everything is evolving, everything is falling apart.

—Tyler Durden in *Fight Club* by Chuck Palahniuk

When I was in my twenties, I made the good choice (one of the few) to take a job as a caregiver and homecare aide for older adults. One woman who I worked with named Elizabeth, affectionately called Betty by her husband, was a devout Catholic. She had a henhouse full of children, grandchildren, and great-grandchildren. She taught Sunday school and knitted blankets for the homeless. Betty's house smelled like Werther's Originals, and I'm pretty sure she owned twelve pink sweatshirts with embroidered cats. Crucifixes were everywhere, naturally.

After learning that I was nearing twenty-six and single (the horror!), she gave me a little glossy card with a picture of St. Jude on the front.

"The patron saint of desperate cases and lost causes," she said and nodded as she handed me the card. I touched its rough edges and put it in the back pocket of my scrubs before setting about giving her husband a bath and scrubbing their kitchen floors until they were "just so," as she peeked around corners and made lingering cups of Folgers coffee.

That evening, when I got back to my single rented place where I petted my single cat as I ate two bowls of cereal for supper, I looked at the picture of St. Jude. He looked a little bit like a thinner Ron Swanson from *Parks and Recreation*, eyes with kind, burly resolve. I am not Catholic, though my grandparents on my mother's side were. I don't pray to saints, though I am of the opinion that if it works, work it (just like we say in recovery).

But I kept Mr. Jude in the inside pocket of my purse for quite a while. Somewhere along the way he got lost, but my memory of this little snip of time did not. I can still see Betty's floral housecoat and curlers, eyes looking at me, the desperately lost cause, with pity and love.

My life was indeed a desperate case—one smothered by addiction, mental health challenges, and undiagnosed trauma symptoms. The kind old woman didn't know a sliver of my reality (if she did, she may have asked to bathe me in holy water).

If you looked at the outer shell of my upbringing, compared to other kids I grew up with, it looked pretty shiny on the outside. And indeed, it was in many respects. I was privileged. I always had enough to eat. Even on my mom's weekends (kids from divorced homes know what I'm talking about). She scrimped and saved so that we had the sugary cereal she let us eat (my dad wouldn't). I had clothes—even if they weren't the trendiest versions (what I wouldn't have given for those jeans with the little green triangle on the butt). There were a handful of family vacations. I even had my own bathroom for God's sake.

Yes, it looked pretty nice on the outside. But inside the doors of my formative years, things weren't so pretty. It's taken me several decades to sort through it all—and be sober-minded enough to do so. I've spent thousands of hours in a therapist's chair, at a hundred bucks a pop, and been to addiction treatment in all its various forms: inpatient and outpatient and intensive outpatient. I've been prayed for, had hands laid on me. I've been the honorary recipient of well-intentioned youth evangelism because of my "at-risk" status (hey, guys!), and more.

I felt like St. Jude's most desperate and pathetic single lady in my midtwenties, all the while dreaming of a white picket fence and dashing tall husband and bobble-headed children, a dream that felt like nothing more than an unimaginable fantasy. Something J. K. Rowling might dream up in her armchair.

Do you have a picture of that life you dreamed of? But maybe instead it was the opposite of what you had at home? Maybe it mirrored a television show where the dad always came home at a certain time and the mom hung the clothes out on the line. Maybe you dreamed (or dream) of some version of a future that had red roses every Valentine's Day and a two-car garage with labeled shelves and containers, making pancakes every Saturday morning for well-behaved ten-year-old concert pianists. Or maybe your dream was or is simply to be loved.

This is the lie that kept me stuck in trauma for years: I was too broken for that life. The one where I was loved well.

I'd experienced too much hurt at the hands of men to lean in to and fully trust one. My temple had been demolished. And what is more, what I knew about marriage freaked me out. It felt more like a live trap or death sentence—not so much a state of being that could actually bring me joy and help me learn more about God and humility and sacrifice and what life is all about.

Love and Marriage

When I was about fourteen or fifteen, right after the first time I was sexually assaulted, I was in so much unprocessed pain that I used to take one of our hard crystal juice glasses into my bedroom and stare into the mirror as I hit myself over and over on the bone outlining my eye socket. I didn't understand why I felt the way I did, why I felt so alone. Desperate. Scared. The sorrow in me making a cavernous, festering, invisible wound. I remember liking the way the glass felt on my face. The burning. It made my pain physical and not so hard to place.

I talk more about my experience of sexual trauma in my first book, *Downstairs Church*. Sexual violence is something that many of us, sadly, have experienced, but don't talk about. For some, the trauma results from years of objectification that begins when puberty hits. Or microaggressions that subtly attack ("You should smile more"; "You look so nice when you wear skirts"). Death by a thousand little cuts.* I recently heard a startling statistic that one in five women are sexually abused as children.

For others, like me, it was a combination of abuses, including rape, that threatened to define my life. Even as a twenty-something doing homecare for older adults, afraid that the life I wanted wasn't possible because of what I'd suffered. Because

---

* This refers to an ancient style of Chinese execution where someone was killed by many small cuts. In this context, it refers to how microaggressions, even though like small cuts, can do immense harm.

my temple had been desecrated, I wasn't worthy of love. I was in love with showing up and loving other people, and at the same time, terrified that I was never going to be lovable myself. I looked into the mirror and hated what I saw.

Do you have these really hard things in your story? Or in your family's story?

Deep breath.

I want to recognize here that this content is jarring. It's tough. Even if you haven't experienced some of the things I talk about, you've no doubt got a little empath in you or you wouldn't be reading this. I encourage you to take breaks when you choose to as you read this book, lean on your people, or read with a small group for support. I'd like to remind you that I also include an appendix in the back that walks you through examples of exercises you can do when the content you are reading is triggering for you.

I didn't know at the time before I was married or had kids (BT—Before Twins, my husband and I joke), how much the trauma can layer on itself and circle round and round like a conch shell. How much what comes before us (even before we were born) impacts our life. And importantly, how all this can affect how we see and treat ourselves and our bodies.

There were other traumas layered on too that you might be able to relate to. I come from a divorced home. When I was growing up, even when I was doing unhealthy things like self-harm or, later, using alcohol and other drugs to escape the pain, I didn't realize how much the divorce of my parents impacted me. Or maybe it isn't divorce but some other major event or past family event that impacted your early life? Whatever your hard thing or "TMT"—The Massive Thing—is, as my friend Dr. Lee

Warren likes to say,[16] you can relate to the devastation of trauma if you didn't have the coping skills or tools to heal from it.

For me, one of the things I've carried from my family tree was the *un*truth that marriage was never something sacred. Or final. It was a contract, not a covenant. Something that could be signed on the dotted line, but if you forgot to cross your t's, or if the date was off by a day, or, as happens after the New Year for me, you accidentally write the year before, it would all be okay because you could just change it. Rip it up. Get out. Trade in for a newer model. But it was trauma that made me think this and distrust the idea of marriage for myself.

> What are your *un*truths that have kept you stuck or keep you stuck today and prevent you from honoring yourself and your story?

So it wasn't any surprise that while most women my age were getting married and having their first or even second babies, I was sitting with my cat at night wondering what I was going to do with my life. My dad would pull me aside at family dinners saying that if I was gay, the family would accept it. I'd tell him I wasn't gay, and he'd sort of look at me like everyone else who found out I was still single. They'd feel sorry for me. They'd pity me. They'd wonder to themselves why a girl like me hadn't found "the one" yet. What was wrong with me? The prevailing question behind their eyes. And mine.

Like Monster, these questions were heavy and stuck around.

I didn't know much about love, except that it was hard. Temporary. Riddled with pain and mistrust and two sides of every story. Love isn't patient, it's hasty. Love isn't kind, it's confused. Jealous. Arrogant. Vengeful. Love seeks after personal happiness and self-actualization. Merely checks the boxes off Maslow's hierarchy of needs.* It's got a short fuse. Keeps a long list of grievances that are aired on Main Street or TikTok. It delights in the downfall of others, runs away, never trusts, never hopes.

Love quits.

What are your own thoughts of love and how has your childhood (or lack thereof) contributed to how you view love, give love, or receive it? So much of our experience today can be connected to what we experience in our past, especially in our childhood and the untruths that followed us—and maybe even our families—for generations.

These aren't comfortable conversations or topics. This is tough.

But remember, in the beginning of this book, I made a weighty promise that we'd move through the tough stuff together to get to a place of greater healing and freedom.

If you are still reading these words, I'd like to encourage you with this:

You've already started taking new steps toward protecting, honoring, and loving yourself. You are facing the tough stuff as you reflect deeply on the questions throughout these chapters.

---

* Maslow's Hierarchy of Needs is a theory in psychology that states there are five stages of human needs that motivate our behavior. From the bottom of the hierarchy and up, the needs are as follows: physiological (food and clothing), safety (job security), love and belonging needs (friendship), esteem, and self-actualization. One of the main principles of the theory is that the lower needs must be met before someone can attend to higher needs.

You are reading bits of my story, likely being reminded of your own. Perhaps God is even bringing new things to mind.

This might feel uncomfortable or even confusing at first. We are talking about trauma and now you want me to write about the things I like or love about my self (you may be asking)? Yes. I want us to quick pivot because both of these things can be true at once.

We can experience trauma and respect ourselves. We can go through hard things and still love ourselves. It might take practice, and you might skip this and keep on reading for now, but I want to encourage you to come back to this place. The place where we begin to have compassion for our stories and can honor our lives.

If you feel comfortable, now is a great time to take out a journal and reflect. Check out my course called Journal Recovery at CarolineBeidler.com, if you'd like to dig deeper into a journaling practice.

Power in a Name

Perhaps you, too, grew up in a broken household, one that was defined by divorce. Or maybe you grew up with an absent parent. Even if living in a blended family brought love and acceptance and presence (like mine did in many ways), maybe you were also led to always feel not good enough. Unwanted. Unloved. Or maybe your family trauma runs deeper and brings with it the complexity of culture and society. Maybe your racial or ethnic identity is woven into a patchwork quilt of trauma that your ancestors experienced: slavery, racism, subjugation, torment. Things that, as a white woman living in privilege, I cannot imagine. There are so many things my bones will never know.

Nona Jones is a woman I found on Instagram. It's sort of strange to say, but maybe not in today's world where we can connect with people on a global scale in new ways just by picking up our phones. The first thing I noticed about Nona (besides her impeccable sense of fashion and transcendent beauty) was the power in her words.

Nona Jones is an international speaker, pastor, and business executive. Pretty sure under the word "diva" in the dictionary, there is a picture of her in a leopard-print pantsuit. Here is a snapshot of her early years:

> When Nona's mother found out she was pregnant with her, she cried. She didn't want the burden of a child, and, even though she was married to Nona's father who wanted a child, she didn't want to be a mother. When Nona's father passed away two months shy of her second birthday, her mother moved to a new state to be with a man she barely knew. After a string of boyfriends over a two-year period, she settled with a guy who became her live-in boyfriend. And that's when the abuse began.[17]

Nona's early years were centered on the feeling of being unwanted and unloved. The love she did eventually come to know as a young child and woman was distorted and sexualized and predatory. No child should ever have to experience what she did.

And yet—

And yet her story is one of redemption and beauty too.

Nona's life is an example of resilience and power. She moved through the pain of her past into new seasons of growth, ministry, and leadership. Now she travels the world sharing about topics that so many women experience, like the harm of comparison, rejection, and trauma. Nona speaks on the dark parts of life from the perspective of someone who has been there. Then she shines the light of a woman who has risen from the ashes.

I don't know Nona personally (though I wish I did!), but her story reminds me that though the pain we experience in our families can be gaping, healing can and does happen. If you've ever fallen on gravel as a kid, you know that fragments of dirt and stone can embed into torn flesh in all kinds of ways. This kind of injury takes time to heal.

Trauma in the Branches of the Family Tree

I am thirteen years old and in the eighth grade when my stomach pain begins. I am going to a Catholic grade school run by Franciscan nuns. The pain starts the night I am to play Mary in the eighth-grade school Christmas play. I feel excited because she is one of the main characters in the play, and I feel honored to have been chosen to represent her. I am very disappointed that night, when I don't feel well enough to go. I worked so hard to memorize all my lines, and the night finally comes.

My whole family goes to see it, but I stay home in bed, everyone thinking I have the flu. Over the next few days, the pain doesn't go away. I have no vomiting or diarrhea, but I am in constant discomfort, with abdominal spasms that come after eating. So I don't eat much to avoid getting the pain.

Because I lose weight quickly, it doesn't take long for me to end up weak and in bed. My face gets thin, and my clothes begin to hang on me, my shoulder blades like a coat hanger.

I never like people focusing on me, no matter how sick I am. I just want to be left alone. But I am constantly asked if I still have the pain. Is it better or worse? Am I feeling sick to my stomach, and does anything make it go away? I tell everyone that nothing makes it feel better, except not eating. I don't have the words to say what is really going on. I'm afraid to talk about what's happening.

I am taken to the local doctor to see if he can find out what is causing my pain. He is handsome with kind eyes. After examining me, he admits he doesn't know the cause. I become more and more discouraged, and my parents become more and more concerned, as no diagnosis is made. I know the doctor is thinking something terrible is wrong because of my rapid weight loss, but none of the tests bring answers. I stay in my bed, eating very little because eating causes the intestinal spasms. I lose thirty pounds. My body shrinks down to eighty-seven pounds, and I go back to wearing children's clothes. I think I am going to die, and so does everyone else, though nobody says it out loud. I have read enough to know that rapid weight loss is one of the symptoms of cancer.

I become intrigued by the process of death and wonder what happens after someone dies. I pore over books about dying children. The children who have died fearlessly are fascinating. I study their process. I read how they suffer, cope so well with the pain, and inspire those around them. I know I can die a heroic death, just like some of them.

I am preparing myself to be like them.

Since my local doctor has not made a diagnosis, my parents take me for a second opinion to a doctor they know in the city. He is the one who delivered me as a baby. I don't like him much. He is an older man with gray hair and a brusque manner. He examines me and says he isn't sure what's wrong. He puts me in the hospital and runs endless blood tests and X-rays. At first, he thinks I have hepatitis, because my liver test results are abnormal. I am put in isolation, all the staff donning gowns, gloves, and masks before coming into my room. It increases my feelings of loneliness but doesn't last long, as the next liver test comes back normal.

A few evenings later, I am lying in my hospital bed while my parents are visiting. I can see the setting sun through my window, and the air in the room is cold. The black telephone on my bedside table rings, and my mother answers it. It is my doctor. I can hear him telling my mother that since all the tests have come back negative, he thinks there might be a psychological reason for my pain. I can hear him suggesting that I see a psychiatrist for a workup and transfer to the psychiatric unit of the hospital. I wish I could tell him.

Mother and Dad agree, not knowing what else to do. I feel so devastated, like nobody believes I have real physical pain, not even my parents. I can't understand why my pain is so hard to diagnose. One of the young hospital interns that I meet that morning comes by my room that night, stands in the doorway in his white coat, and reassures me that everything will be all right. I can tell by the way he talks that he cares about me. I tell him that I hope so. I lie awake most of the night, huddled in a tiny ball in the middle of my hospital bed, worried about what tomorrow will bring.

The next morning, I wake from a nearly sleepless night, exhausted and scared. A nurse comes into my room and tells me that I am soon going to be transferred to the psychiatric unit in the hospital. I appreciate the compassion in her eyes as she tells me.

My parents come early to be with me when I am transferred. They follow the nurse as she wheels me down the hall. We
go up the elevator and stop in front of a locked door. It looks and
feels ominous. It is a locked unit, which I take to mean that
everyone there is either dangerous or wants to escape.

She unlocks and opens the door, and we enter the unit. It is
sparsely decorated and has small tables and chairs placed strategically around the room. On one side is the enclosed nursing
station. I see some patients, mostly middle-aged or older, pacing
constantly back and forth, talking incoherently, or both. Others
don't seem to talk at all but just sit and stare straight ahead.
Most of them are dressed in regular street clothes. Almost
nobody appears normal, in my opinion. Most of them look scary,
with dead-looking eyes that indicate to me that nobody is inside.
I wonder why the doctor feels I need to be here, since I'm not
anything like them.

Before I can fully take it all in, I am taken to my room,
where I unpack my belongings. The nurse instructs me to go
back to the dayroom, where the majority of the patients are,
when everything is put away. I can tell by the look on my parents' faces that they, too, are shocked and apprehensive. I sit
there quietly while my parents talk to each other a bit. When
they leave, I cry. I never go to the dayroom. The nurse finally
comes and gets me and kindly shows me where I can sit. She
says she'll help me and tell me what I am supposed to do, and
when and how to do it.

While I am a patient, I sit huddled at a corner table of the
dayroom watching everyone. There is another young girl like me.

Sara is rather quiet with staff but very friendly to me. She
is about my age, thin, with long blond hair. I envy her hair, since

mine has been cut short for a long time. We stick together as much as we can, since there are so few young people here. Sara loves to draw, so we spend our free time doing pencil drawings of people's faces. She has an artist's notebook, which she shares with me. I get many pointers on how to draw faces, since I have never drawn before. She can draw from memory, but I always need a picture or a real person to duplicate. To my surprise, Sara says I do a good job. She says my finished pictures resemble the people I am attempting to draw. I take pride in that, for I've never considered myself an artist.

Sara and I don't talk about why we are there. She doesn't ask me and I don't ask her. I hear someone say she attempted suicide, but that doesn't matter to me. All I know is that I have fun with her, and she is more like me than anyone else here. We spend hours in occupational therapy, making leather wallets and gluing mosaic tiles on little pieces of wood. Sara and I aren't sure what this has to do with being in the psychiatric unit and getting better, but we don't mind. It is something to do besides watching the strange people.

We also spend time in group therapy, as they call it. We are supposed to talk about our problems, but we don't say much. When we are alone, we talk mainly about art and other things. It gets our minds off being there and makes me feel kind of normal.

My psychiatrist is a short, middle-aged, somber man who never smiles and seldom speaks. He wears a suit with his tie half undone, or else wears a baggy sweater that isn't in style. I notice he likes wearing different shades of brown, which I think is rather boring. I don't like him much. I sit in my chair facing him during my daily therapy sessions, and we often sit in silence.

I think he is supposed to be doing most of the talking, so I wait for him to ask me some questions. The one question he does ask me over and over again is, "Why are you depressed?" And I give him the same answer each time: "I'm depressed because I'm sick." I am very frustrated with him! We go in circles. I can't see the purpose of it. It doesn't make me feel any better.

I see the statement he writes: "Only on rare occasions is she able to smile." The psychiatric test results indicate that I have chosen to "be a good girl at all costs" and have "repressed anger." I have "emotional issues" and am diagnosed with "depression and anorexia." He writes hardly any notes during our sessions, and I'm sure that's because we don't talk. In my mind, there is nothing for him to write about.

The therapy sessions with the psychiatrist get me nowhere, and I feel the same as I did when I was first admitted. I have my stomach pain and eat very little. I am given some medications, which don't make me feel any different. One day my parents tell me that the psychiatrist has suggested shock treatments. They tell me they are given for depression that doesn't respond to other treatment. The hope is that I forget why I am depressed and get well. Since I am only thirteen, my parents give permission for the treatments. I don't have anything to say about it. Everyone is hopeful that they will work. I don't know what to think.

The day for my first treatment comes. I am very nervous, not knowing what to expect. Early that morning, the staff puts me in a hospital gown and lays me on a padded treatment table covered with a sheet. The psychiatrist explains to me that I will get some medication and go to sleep. He says I will wake up in a little while and will not remember some things. After he finishes talking, staff hold down my arms and body and my head swims. I feel something go into my mouth, and then I am asleep.

The next thing I know, I wake up, not knowing where I am or what is going on. I don't recognize the room. I look at my roommate, a little white-haired lady who had a treatment that morning. I can't ask her where I am. She is confused too. She has a dazed look on her face, staring at nothing, lying there motionless. It is a horrible feeling, not remembering anything. We both just lie there quietly trying to remember something, anything, until a nurse finally comes in. It feels like we have been lying there for hours. She gets us out of bed and helps us dress, then we sit across from each other in the dayroom. Still confused, I try to look like I know what is going on, but I don't. Our lunch stares back in silence. I crouch down in my chair, trying to make myself small. I worry my memory won't come back. What will I do then?

Most of my memory comes back over the next few days. It is difficult though, for as soon as I begin to remember, it is the day for another treatment. Sometimes the treatments work, the doctors say, but they don't work for me. My medical record states that I have eight treatments "given without benefit." There are only a few of us on the unit who get these treatments, but most of the other people who get them are old. At least they all have white hair, so I think they are old. I can always tell who they are, because they are the ones who look lost and confused on the same days I am. It is hard for me to tell if these people get any better. Maybe they look at me and try to figure out the same thing? I don't know. Or maybe they just don't care. I know I feel sorry for them.

There is a young nurse who works the day shift in the psychiatric unit who lives in my hometown. I am afraid she will tell people in town that I am in the psychiatric unit and have been given shock treatments. I am deeply ashamed about being here. Being physically sick is acceptable, but to have mental or emotional issues is not okay. I know it will give people in town something new to gossip about. I don't know what my parents are telling their friends about me. I never ask. I am depressed, but no one ever asks why.

—Mother

Chapter 4

Inching Toward Freedom

I got braver like a crab going sideways. I inched towards courage . . .
—Julia Alvarez, *In the Time of the Butterflies*

My hubby once bought me a steam cleaner so I could go slowly from room to room deep cleaning our house. I was psyched! I never thought I would be the kind of woman to get excited over household cleaning gadgets, but I am. Getting rid of the remnants of my traumatic past and breaking free from the brokenness in my family has been just like this: going room to room, issue to issue, and cleaning house.

The dog smell circulates through the plastic gadgets, and the smell of hair-clumped soap reminds me why I don't like having indoor pets. They leave their mark everywhere. In my mind, I hear the country song "Bless the Broken Road," and I have to laugh as I think, *God bless this steam-cleaned mess.*

Have you ever poured out what steam cleaners suck out of even seemingly clean carpets? It is horrendous and smelly and dark like chocolate pudding. It's astounding how much dirt is trapped in the bristly fibers of taupe carpeting circa 1990.

The stuff I've dredged from the remnants of my past has been equally disgusting. And tough. This is one of the most challenging things for anyone working through trauma: to be confronted with reality—especially when this reality is not as glittery or filtered as it appears on Instagram. We can be not only confronted but pushed, stretched to the edge of what we think we are capable of.

So how can we practically move into the new? How do we heal? What role can we play in the miraculous change of our own heart and mind? And what about our spirit? Is transformation even possible?

I asked myself the same questions that day during graduate school when I paused on my bike as a moving bus approached. While I contemplated ending it all, the supernatural power of God swooped in. I didn't realize at the time how ready I was to receive it (again). I made it through that experience—thoughts of suicide—like so many of the things I'd lived through. But I had more questions at that time than answers.

Brené Brown says that cultivating hope, practicing critical awareness, and letting go of numbing are elements that make up resilient people.[18] Amazing. I love it. I want to type this up and print it off and hang it on my bathroom mirror and say mantras to my reflection as I'm putting on my deodorant like "you are hopeful, you are present, you are free," etc. Maybe I just will. I also agree with her point that practicing critical awareness or coming to know ourselves is important. In knowing ourselves—or at least committing to getting to know ourselves, we are honoring ourselves too.

While all this might be helpful, what I really want to know is *how*. How do we cultivate resilient spirit? How, as it relates to our trauma, whatever that may be, do we move on from it to get to a place of being able to feel all the things and yet still get out of bed in the morning with a genuine smile and an honest eagerness to show up for the people we love? How can we love and show up for ourselves after what we've been through? How can we break free from our family's history of trauma? How can we be walking, breathing change in our lineages and family trees?

Answers from the Broken Road

When I was in the middle of a horribly tough breakup with my ex-fiancé, after I had fallen deep in sleepy love with him and his parents and their hippy Lutheran church and his five-year-old angelic son, I needed some rescue. Trying to wade through the grief of heartache is devastating and gave me an emotional hangover like when drinking one too many bottles of sparkling Lambrusco. I longed for love and security and stability, and while I knew he wasn't the path I was supposed to be walking, a part of me wished it could be so. Why couldn't my very human attempt at love pave itself into a path of life that was simple and sturdy?

Why couldn't I clear my own path? Or why couldn't I rely on someone else—a man—to do this for me?

After leaving him and breaking off the engagement at a ripe twenty-two years old, I cried myself to sleep every night and woke up on a soggy pillow. I hope you didn't know this was actually a thing, sweet reader: waking up crying. It is.

I agonized as I tried to leave for weeks, then did, then kept seeing him at my new apartment, kept trying to make up reasons why I had to leave. Imagining myself Emily Dickinson's modern, more morose cousin. I wrote dull, passive, flowery lines in an old notebook:

One single tear—
That had been waiting.
Kissing my cheek.
Salt water burning raw skin.
The pain
deep
a
slice
into
heaven.

But I knew I was supposed to leave. We had grown apart— and I was too young.

He wasn't the one. Or two.

I set a loving boundary and practiced loving, protecting, and honoring myself.

There were several lines in the sand after him (not telling numbers, friends)—lines that I couldn't create or uphold, but wanted to. The line that trauma had distorted and stolen from me, that a grisly series of men bruised and broke down without even a word. Mr. Wrong-for-Me's who I wanted to tell so much truth to but instead became immobilized like an unsocialized cat. Crouching, staring, a stone-terror statue in all my unhealthy attempts at relationships. From trauma came a series of unhealthy relationships with which I, without boundaries, des-ecrated the temple of my being.

Looking back now, I have empathy for that young twenty-something so thirsty for love, who thought she was doing the hardest thing she had ever done by leaving. Since then, I've done countless "hardest things" and cried so many tears, some because of my trauma recovery and some just because I'm human. But the truth is now, where I am standing today with a little family of my own, having done things that never would have been done had I stayed, it makes sense. But I'm going to be real with you: it hasn't been easy.

Setting boundaries and learning that I'm worth it has taken practice. For me, and so many of the people I've worked with and learned from, it has been a series of practice sessions. Similar to how runners don't just go out and run a marathon, we need to practice setting boundaries mile by mile. When I started recovery from my alcohol and drug addiction, it allowed me the space (and clearheadedness) to think through my decisions. Day by day, I began to see that the series of unhealthy relationships and my unhealthy choices needed to be uprooted first by looking inward.

Protect the Temple with a Wall

The phrase "self-care" has a hint of wrongness about it, like someone needs to update their messaging. I'm sure you've heard it somewhere before. Greedily reading it in *People* magazine at the dentist's office, hearing it at your therapist's office, or seeing it on Instagram. Wherever you've heard it, you might be like me and utterly done with it. Annoyed even. Sometimes these societal buzzwords seem so true and so right, but they eventually get overused and the meaning suddenly loses value like the latest cryptocurrency. Overuse can even happen with the word *love*.

Just think of this sentence: I *love* good, old-fashioned Southern macaroni and cheese. And I also love my kids. My best friend.

My favorite teal nightshirt with the words "mama bear" on it. My sexy, yard-working, Wrangler-wearing husband. It's ridiculous that we have one word for all these precious things that have varying degrees of lovability. For example, I love my kids and husband much more than I love mac and cheese (most days).

The imagery surrounding self-care is outdated too. Milky warm baths with books and sparkling water (or wine) on HomeGoods ads. Or the less sedentary and finger-pruning pictures, like running through a lush forest, adrenaline releasing like pine needles in late summer.

Even though research shows that movement and exercise can repair harm done by trauma to our nervous system (I'm a huge proponent of not only baths but exercise too), there must be more to self-care. And there must be more to healing than being wrapped in a monogrammed towel (that I've never been wealthy enough to think to buy).

But boundaries take the concept of self-care in the right direction.

Choosing to leave my ex-fiancé was one of the first times I practiced drawing a loving line in the sand—for myself. Having healthy boundaries is one important way to extend self-love and care to ourselves. I've learned this firsthand—but not, of course, from having stellar boundaries my whole life. There was a time when I had *zero* boundaries.

It didn't matter if it had to do with work, school, or relationships, I've been a flimsy doormat. Because of the trauma I experienced in the past, along with a number of other reasons (we'll get to these later), my sense of self was very distorted. I didn't know how to and was not able to create and maintain my own boundaries.

I know many people, especially women, who struggle with boundary issues. Just google the topic and almost four hundred million search results pop up! Clearly, this is something that is on a lot of people's minds and something that is important to address. In our self-obsessed culture, too, there is a fascination with anything that will minimize interaction with others. But there is a difference between being called to selflessness and allowing ourselves to be taken advantage of or outright harmed. Protecting our temples is where the real love is. This is part of the "how" of dealing with trauma we carry.

In order to explore this topic further, first I'd like to delve into what boundaries are. Then, let's look at some healthy ways to set up boundaries (and maybe I'll throw in some examples from my past that are of the "what not to do" variety). So here we go.

What Are Boundaries?

I love this definition from a mental health treatment center in Australia, the Resilience Centre:

> Personal boundaries are guidelines, rules, or limits that a person creates to identify reasonable, safe, and permissible ways for other people to behave toward them and how they will respond when someone passes those limits. They are built out of a mix of conclusions, beliefs, opinions, attitudes, past experiences, and social learning. Personal boundaries help to define an individual by outlining likes and dislikes and setting the distances one allows others to approach. Boundaries are essential to healthy relationships and, really, a

healthy life. Setting and sustaining boundaries is a skill.[19]

Boundaries are really all about self-worth or how much we value ourselves. When we love and value ourselves, we set up healthy boundaries out of respect for ourselves. When we don't value who we are or don't feel like we deserve respect, we look to others to define and set our boundaries for us, which isn't good for anyone.

In a healthy and vibrant recovery, creating personal boundaries is a basic life skill that is so important; it teaches us to respect our temples, promotes self-care, and communicates to those around us how we feel about ourselves. Boundaries also let others know not only how we want to be treated but what we will tolerate and where we draw the line. In order to make recovery shine, learning to set up healthy boundaries is something we can practice.

For me, this wasn't an innate skill. I needed to learn and practice this over time. What helped me the most was coming to understand my true worth and value as a woman. Not because of anything I've done (or not done) but simply because I was created—and created by a God who loves me.

Here's a fun list of all the ways I've had very unhealthy boundaries in the past. Can you relate?

- Not knowing who I am or having a flimsy sense of my own identity or selfhood
- Oversharing very intimate details about myself or my past in unsafe spaces
- Not expressing my true needs and wants
- Allowing others to make decisions for me

- Not taking responsibility for my own choices or life direction
- Getting self-worth (or lack thereof) from how I'm treated by others

According to the Resilience Centre, healthy boundaries allow an individual to:

- Foster a strong sense of self-worth and self-regard
- Gradually disclose personal information within the context of a trusting and reciprocal relationship
- Safeguard both your physical and emotional space against unwarranted intrusion
- Cultivate an equitable partnership where responsibilities and power are shared
- Practice assertiveness by confidently expressing both affirmative and negative responses, and accepting others' negative responses gracefully
- Differentiate your needs, thoughts, feelings, and desires from those of others, recognizing the uniqueness of your boundaries and requirements
- Empower yourself to make healthful choices and take accountability for your well-being; in situations involving physical danger or threats, seeking support from a counselor, therapist, or advocate is advisable to create a safety plan, which may involve establishing clear boundaries

That's a big list. It takes work and practice. And what is more, having healthy boundaries is all about recognizing that we have the right to be treated well. This might sound simple, but for many of us with addiction and other co-occurring challenges, this is a lesson hard learned. Many of us have experienced so many boundary violations it is a miracle that we are still standing—that our bodies have any edge, any outline about them at all. It's a miracle our flesh hasn't disintegrated into someone else, that person everyone wants us to be.

So how can we practice healthy boundaries?

A practical way to practice healthy boundaries is through assertive communication. This communication style is a skill and can be learned if you are like me and communication hasn't come naturally and has been influenced by trauma. Being assertive in communication expresses to others that you respect yourself enough to share your opinions and thoughts, and to stand up for your beliefs. Importantly, it is also done in a way that respects others' viewpoints. The Mayo Clinic has some excellent tips on how to practice being assertive in communication.[20]

- Practice saying no or sharing your opinion in low-stress situations (like when picking a restaurant with friends)
- Practice or write down conversations that may feel tough (it's okay to rehearse!)
- Use "I feel . . ." statements when in a conflict or high-stress situation
- Ask for help or backup (there is no shame in asking someone you trust to practice a tough conversation or saying no)

Establishing healthy boundaries has been tough for me over the years. I've struggled with feeling like I don't have much agency or choice in my own life. Learning to develop boundaries—whether that is with romantic relationships, friendships, people I'm working with, or even my own time— has been life-changing. By being able to say no and prioritize my own care, I can show up for myself and others in a healthier and more loving way.

Ultimately, when we communicate in a direct and assertive way, we are communicating to others that we respect ourselves and value our own thoughts and opinions. It may not happen overnight, but practicing being assertive can really pay off in the long run and help to make our recoveries shine.

> Is there a boundary you need to set? What does it look like to draw a figurative line in the sand?

We indeed may all be tired of the phrase "self-care," but it is wrapped in truth. To care and love ourselves, to communicate to others our wants and needs and desires, even sharing how we want to be treated, is such a beautiful and precious gift. Protecting the temple and honoring the self by committing to greater levels of self-awareness and boundary setting can set us on a path toward greater healing. One of the many paths that God brings to healing trauma. All we need to do is walk it.

> Five Actions You Can Take: Protect the Temple
>
> - Be kind to yourself (take a break, a walk, a rest).
> - Say no to a thing—*anything*—that deserves a no from you (this could be a person, place, thing, request, or even one of your own ideas).

- Try learning assertive communication (and see how you feel).
- Write yourself a love letter (sounds cheesy, but think of a couple things that you love about yourself and why). This will remind you of the beauty of the temple you are trying to protect.
- Finish this journal prompt:

  I feel most protected and loved when . . .

Rhythm 2

Practice Forgiveness—Radical Compassion

Chapter 5

Understanding Adverse Childhood Experiences

This morning the redbirds' eggs
have hatched [. . .] they know nothing
about the sky that's waiting. Or
the thousands, the millions of trees.
They don't even know they have wings. [. . .]

—"This Morning" by Mary Oliver

Another one of my exes—I'll call him Mr. Big—had casual long-sleeved button-up shirts like my dad. One that I loved to wear was soft yellow-and-gray plaid and covered all parts of me. If I had a look back then, it would have been vagabond chic. The only clothes I felt comfortable in were clothes like this or baggy sweatshirts. I hated shorts (my thighs were too big) and I hated tight dresses (I was so big-boned) and I hated low-cut blouses (I was too flat chested). Think: the opposite of body positivity. But even if I'd had the body I thought I wanted back then, I would have tried anything to cover it up. I hated being looked at. I never wanted to be seen.

Mr. Big moved into the city with his mom after he gradu-
ated from high school (I was still a couple years behind). I'd go
and stay with him as much as I could, even if that meant (and
it usually meant) watching him and his friends play video
games and smoke ridiculous amounts of cannabis. I could
drink as much as I wanted there and I could smoke as much as
I wanted there. His friends were annoying and thought I was
a "mooch," but I was sadly used to that. Like a barnacle or
some other kind of fungus, I clung to whatever or whoever
could satiate my longing to escape. Mr. Big had a brother who
worked at a liquor store, so there were always bottles of gin
and joints and mushrooms or whatever else we all felt like
doing for fun on the weekends. It all seemed normal—the
using.

What wasn't normal was what happened when everyone
left. He would get angry and we would get drunker. I'd claw
into the details of the room to distract myself. The white noise
of the large fan plugged in by the door. The soft plush black
comforter. The acidic caramel smell of Captain Morgan. The
over-stuffed pillows. A poster of Tyra Banks in braids stepping
out of a pool to stare back at me. I could almost make out her
shape in the dark as I focused my vision and tried to be anywhere but there.

This was normal, right? Being degraded for someone
else's pleasure. Never getting any pleasure myself. Only emp-
tiness and a dreamy fog—when I even remembered. Many
were the glassy moments of blackouts and dissociation. These
were aftershocks of what I didn't know at the time was
trauma.

Not your typical after-school days and high school weekends for a sixteen-year-old. Like the birds in Mary Oliver's poem, back then I didn't know I even had wings.

Unsafe in My Own Body

Years later, when I was in my early twenties, I noticed a red mark on the bottom of my foot, like an old callous that would not go away. At night, I'd fidget and scratch the bottom of my foot in precisely that one rugged spot. Over the span of a couple days or maybe it was months—who really knows, I was still using drugs at that point—I had scraped so much and so pointedly in that one spot that there was something, I noticed, peeking out.

There was something in there, in my foot. Was it a wart? I'd had warts on my sole before. Maybe this was the same thing, I recall thinking.

Self-surgical procedures fascinated me. In middle school, I pierced my belly button with a safety pin and an ice cube. So, I continued digging with tweezers and then the sharp end of an old-school nail file. (By the way: do not try this at home, please—none of these tools were sterile. And I realize how neurotic this all sounds. Is it less strange if I tell you how stoned I was?)

Eventually, after my delicate digging, there was something I could grab with my thumb and pointer finger. I pulled and pulled and then lifted something right out of the pad of my foot: a one-and-a-half-inch piece of glass. There was minimal blood. This thing had been embedded for God knows how long.

I stared at this little piece of glass in both horror and amazement.

Somehow, I had gotten by, limping along, without the faintest notion that this strange thing had happened. At some point earlier on, I had stepped on glass. I learned how to adapt, to accommodate it. The pain disappearing into my flesh the more I walked on.

In the years between that moment of self-surgery and today, I learned more about the trauma my mother experienced as a child. After those events in the psychiatric unit, she struggled with eating disorders, relationship problems, and other addictions. Can it be a coincidence that my mother and I have experienced so much of the same trauma and so many of the same aftershocks? Would I have experienced the life I have if she could have gotten help and healing earlier on in her life? Would she have married my father in the first place? Would I even be here? Would I have spent so much time with Mr. Big?

From family members, I've heard pieces of stories: what it's been like to be hungry during the Depression or what it was like to watch the planes get shot down over France during WWII or how when someone close to you violates you it dissolves any sense of safety or stability. I know that you and your family have your stories too. We could get lost together, you and I, I'm sure of it—in the grit of trauma and its retelling—if we had a cup of coffee together. This friendly meeting would most certainly need a trigger warning. Perhaps a nice long counseling session after.

The vines of trauma can linger for years, reaching into our hearts and choking out the light. Dr. Bessel van der Kolk wrote:

Traumatized people chronically feel unsafe inside their bodies: The past is alive in the form of gnawing interior discomfort. Their bodies are constantly bombarded by visceral warning signs, and, in an attempt to control these processes, they often become expert at ignoring their gut feelings and in numbing awareness of what is played out inside. They learn to hide from their selves.[21]

Regardless of how trauma or family trauma impacts us today, research shows how it can impact how we feel. Whether we feel safe or not. Loved or not. Present or not. It can impact our ability to have compassion for ourselves and to forgive.

Let's take a moment to notice: what is coming up for you right now?

For me, when I reflect on the hard parts of my story, sometimes I feel sadness and sometimes I feel compassion.

How are you feeling at this point in the book?

I'd like to remind you that there is an appendix that is there for you if you have moments of feeling triggered or need to pause. I also want to encourage you to reach out for support or to talk with someone you trust about what might be coming up for you. Part of the journey toward healing and self-compassion can be uncomfortable and even downright painful. We don't have to go on this journey alone.

Virginia Creeper

Trauma is like the invasive species of plant with five leaves that stretch out like star limbs. Virginia creeper crawls up almost every living tree in East Tennessee. My husband says it is impossible to get rid of this plant after it appears, yet it needs to be destroyed, otherwise the damage will be too great. Otherwise, he'll have to (gladly) get the chainsaw out and start cutting things down.

If I stare out one of our windows, I can see Virginia creeper everywhere on the mountain trees. It reminds me of the concept of "adverse childhood experiences" or ACEs. According to the Center for Disease Control and Prevention, these are "potentially traumatic events that occur in childhood (zero to seventeen years), events like experiencing violence, abuse, or neglect; witnessing violence in the home or community; having a family member attempt or die by suicide. Also included are aspects of the child's environment that can undermine their sense of safety, stability, and bonding, such as growing up in a household with: substance use problems, mental health problems, and/or instability due to parental separation or household members being in jail or prison."[22]

In other words, ACEs are just that: anything that happens in childhood that's tough and may be traumatic. Now importantly, ACEs have been studied by researchers since the 1990s, and some interesting (but not surprising) results have surfaced. The more ACEs someone has (or the higher their ACE score), the more other outcomes (that aren't so great) happen later in life. Problems with relationships, substance misuse, mental illness, and even chronic health issues like heart disease can result.

Having bad things happen in childhood is not uncommon. If you are still reading, you know this. One study notes that about 61 percent of adults report that they have experienced at least one type of ACE, and nearly one in six reported they have experienced four or more types of ACEs. Notably (though again, not surprisingly), women and people of color are at greater risk for having experienced four or more varieties of ACEs.[23]

We are not alone.

Sadly, most people in recovery that I've met (and perhaps you too) score off the charts with ACEs. It's not a matter of one or two experiences labeled "adverse"; the reality is that the number is in the tens or twenties by the time many of us reach college.

There has been quite a bit of research done on ACEs. What makes ACEs so tough is the fact that these childhood experiences began long before we were even a thought in our parents' minds. A lineage of trauma can creep up the trees of our family histories, slowly wreaking havoc, choking out the light. What is more? Oftentimes, while ACEs are better acknowledged in conversations today, especially among therapists and researchers, what is missing is an important follow-up: What's next? How do we prevent our ACEs from becoming our AAEs (adverse adulthood experiences)?

When these bad/hard/tough/excruciating/horrible things happen, how can we move through them into a place of forgiveness and radical compassion? Not just for the perpetrators of some of these traumas, but for ourselves?

My own mother's experience (and perhaps her family's before her) created a ripple effect. Whether my trauma was inherited from hers, or passed down because of environmental factors (like how she was able to be there, or not, for my brother and me), or even originated because of a spiritual connection to brokenness that's tied to my lineage, whatever the reason, *there is good news*. We can forgive and we can move into a place of radical compassion. I'll get to that, so let's keep on.*

---

* I want to acknowledge here that while I will continue discussing forgiveness and radical compassion because they are central to the framework I am proposing, forgiving doesn't have to mean forgetting. It is okay to also not be ready to forgive. Recovery is a process, and we are all walking our own path. I want to continue to encourage you to reach out for support locally as well. Reading this book in community is recommended. This is tough content! I am so very proud of you for sticking with it!

Interlude 2

Ripple Effects

I have to get away today. In the pasture below the barn. If I go out the back door of the house down the small gravel road to the barn, the pasture is only a few minutes beyond. It isn't that far away, but far enough so that I can feel.

I lie on the ground, the grass cradling my body. The smell of the earth comforting me. There is the faint smell of manure. My spot is near one of the paths the animals take every day. Today, the nearby cows glance at me and then ignore me. They've seen me here so many times before. I hear a bird's cry circle in the distance, as if its trill is caught in the breeze.

There is no fence separating the cows and me. They just keep grazing, their tails flicking off flies. I look up at the tree that has become so familiar to me. It is stately and majestic, standing alone. I am not sure what kind it is and know only that it isn't an evergreen.

I know every branch, some low hanging and others so far above my head I can hardly see them. The whole tree is beautiful to me. There are some green leaves, but I focus on the branches that have very few leaves. Those are the branches that have become brown, withered. Some have started to die, and others are already dead. I notice that some of them have fallen since the last time I've been there. Is it dying? Slowly? Or is it fighting to live, like me?

I remember the hospital. I think of Sara, the girl I met there like me.

Is she okay?

Does she live on a farm too, and is she back to having the fields and the sunsets as her friends?

Does she wonder what happened to her? That she feels so different, so dirty, so alone?

Does she wonder why?

I look up the hill toward the barn. The white paint on the old wood is melting into the ground around it.

Sometimes I wonder what's happened and if I am dreaming. A waking nightmare.

As if it is someone else's life.

I think back to my return to school. Since I hadn't finished the year, I had to retake that grade again. Now my former friends are ahead of me and I have to make new friends.

All I want to do is hide away.

I can tell sometimes people hesitate when I walk by. I hope they will stop but they keep walking. So I keep walking too.

I look for girls in my new class, ones who are walking the halls alone like me.

They are usually unpopular, for reasons that aren't always clear. Some wear out-of-style clothes. Some break unspoken rules. Maybe some speak up at the wrong time or laugh when something isn't funny. Some look different.

It doesn't seem fair to me that some of us get walked by. Who decides these rules? But who am I to speak up?

I first see Linda in one of my classes. She stands out from the rest of the girls and her entrance into the room reminds me of a quirky movie star. She flounces through the doorway, brown curls bouncing.

She's wearing a colorful yellow dress that rests mid-calf. Her demeanor is confident.

I watch as she raises her hand, asks questions, laughs.

She doesn't seem to care that some of the other girls are whispering, making fun of her. The boys are watching.

She goes on raising her hand and watching the teacher like she is really listening. Like she wants to learn. Like she owns herself.

She acts the way I feel inside but don't have the courage to be.

After class, I linger by the door and Linda says hi. We become friends.

I wonder if Sara has made friends. Or is she alone? Does she have a Linda, someone she wants to become? A woman with a voice?

—Mother

Chapter 6

If God Is Good, Then Why Did This Happen?

Adversity is the first path to truth.

—Lord Byron

Wandering the aisles of a bookstore used to be a daunting task for me. I prefer to purchase books from the comfort of my sofa (in sweatpants) on a quiet Saturday afternoon. It is much easier to find the "best spiritual book of 2021" from a stranger's review on Goodreads than by running my hands down rainbows of spines.

I also struggle with this concept of faith. I've learned out of necessity to be selective when it comes to whom I trust and which of the many stories I believe. And the concept of spiritual formation? The idea that our souls or spirits can develop through pain and repetition the way we build muscles? This concept sometimes feels as far away as the memory of slugging down Boone's Farm Strawberry Hill wine by the riverbank at fourteen.

Long before shopping online was such a thing (and no, I am not a dinosaur, thank you very much), I discovered Philip Yancey. In an instant, I fell in love with his journalistic realism and pragmatic faith. That's the kind of writing I love best: the real. Truth like poetry. I found him around the same time I discovered some of my other favorite authors. I soon realized that being a Christian wasn't something that made my world smaller (as I had been told during my undergrad); it could be a worldview that opened my eyes to new and beautiful ways that I could relate with the world. The way of Jesus brings more, not less, to this strange life.

Finding books reveals new realities and at the same time is intimate, like the warm hug of a dear friend. Do you have books like this? Words that stir something inside you that is tough to explain? Like when you have a friend and they say something at just the right moment in just the right way, and it is like when your eyes look up and you just happen to catch a glimpse of a shooting star?

It wasn't until years later that I realized one of the reasons I connected with Yancey so much: he saw himself much in the same way I do. In his book *Soul Survivor*, he writes, "I have clung fiercely to the stance of a pilgrim, for that is all I am. I have no religious sanction. I am neither pastor nor teacher, but an ordinary pilgrim, one person among many on a spiritual search."[24]

And more than this, Mr. Yancey just happened to write books like *Where Is God When it Hurts?*, *Unhappy Secrets of the Christian Life*, and *Disappointment with God*. Books with topics that were questions that consumed me for a long time. Things I thought people who go to church didn't like to talk about.

In particular, one of his books struck me like a lightning flash and covered the topic that I was most curious about getting answers for: pain.

Pain was the thing I could not reconcile. Not in my own life and not in the world around me. And I did not have the luxury of distraction so readily at my fingertips (this was long before TikTok, people).

If God was good, then *why*?

Why was my life so messed up? Why was pain my only friend? How could I ever forgive the people in my life who had hurt me?

Maybe you can relate. Maybe you have questions and doubts about a faith you have a hard time believing in when you look around or pick up your phone or remember back to *that time when* . . . I've been there.

Buzzkill

When I was sixteen years old, I spent most of my time trying to get high. Anything to help me get my body back to equilibrium. I did not know at the time my entire system was flushed with cortisol; it was as if I was operating on overdrive round-the-clock. Of course, at the time I didn't realize that my needing to self-medicate with any substance I could get my hands on (usually illegal ones) was a coping mechanism for the sexual violence I'd experienced and all the other quiet traumas. It was a way to numb what I didn't even know at the time was likely the aftershocks of my family trauma too. The patterns of coping, addiction, and unhealthy relationships were a mirror that, when I held it up in front of my face, reflected back to me a shadow of my mother.

My sweet little self was just trying to get by. Trying to heal in my own way.

On one particularly sunny afternoon, my boyfriend at the time and I were driving around. Let me just say here that teenagers who get high spend a lot of time in the car. I am speaking from experience. Anyway, it was after a couple day bender of ecstasy and cocaine. I felt like I got hit by a train. For real. My body throbbed. Muscles screamed, pulsating across my puffy forehead, through my nose, raw and red. My shirt was stained from nose bleeds. All I could manage, in all the unmanageability (have you been there?), was smoking menthol cigarettes and staring out the car window (did I mention teens spend time in cars?) and cursing the sun that mocked me with its golden light.

After realizing we weren't going to get any more drugs (a devastating feeling for those in addiction), I held back as long as I could and then watched in the passenger mirror as tears rolled down my swollen face one by one. Cigarette smoke mixed with snot.

I turned my attention toward God. It had been awhile.

"God, if you are really here, I wouldn't feel like this."

No answer.

"If there is a God, why am I in so much pain?"

Silence.

"God?"

Nothing.

Where *was* God when it hurt?

Well, this was precisely the question I wanted answered.

Philip Yancey asks what my sixteen-year-old self was beginning to grapple with in that moment: "if God has the ability to act fairly, speak audibly, and appear visibly, why, then, does he seem so reluctant to intervene today?"[25]

The Purpose of Pain

When Yancey was writing his famous book, *Where Is God When It Hurts?*, he discovered a doctor in India named Dr. Paul Brand who helped him uncover some life- and faith-changing things about pain.

Dr. Paul Brand was a child of missionary parents and later moved back to India after medical school to teach in the late 1940s. He was challenged by a colleague to use his orthopedic skills to help address a horrific result of leprosy: the deforming of the hands and feet. At that time, little was known about this mysterious disease that had such biblical connotations. According to the International Leprosy Association, "it was generally believed that the hands and feet of infected people simply disintegrated or rotted away as a direct result of the disease."[26]

Dr. Brand was one of the leading voices championing research for people, including children, with leprosy at that time. Not surprisingly, he faced much resistance to his work because those with leprosy were stigmatized, often shunned, by their families and society. Dr. Brand, using what he learned working with veterans from WWII and polio patients, came up with a new theory. He discovered that the deformities weren't caused by the disease itself but by infections. Leprosy is a disease of the nervous system. Injuries occurred when his patients couldn't feel pain. The injuries weren't treated because they couldn't be felt and then would get infected and cause innumerable problems.

Dr. Brand created a new "system of pain" for his patients and, as a skilled orthopedic surgeon, developed tendon-transfer techniques that changed hundreds of thousands of people's lives. In many of his books, Yancey talks in-depth about his interviews with Dr. Brand and what he learned from him. They even co-wrote a few books together. Dr. Brand and his research had a profound impact on Yancey and, in an unexpected way, opened up a new door, or perhaps an old door in a new way: Pain has a purpose.

He writes of Brand:

> He invited me to consider an alternative world without pain. He insisted on pain's great value, holding up as proof the terrible results of leprosy—damaged faces, blindness, and loss of fingers, toes, and limbs—all of which occur as side effects of painlessness.[27]

Dr. Brand helped Yancey understand the value of pain in a new way. It was a picture of the redemption of his own pain.

While ACEs and AAEs can have detrimental and spiritually exhausting effects on our lives, pain has value in that it shows there is a way to rise above the trauma and heal. There is a way that God transforms ACEs into and for our good. Dr. Brand learned this. Philip Yancey learned this. You and I can learn this too.

The Apostle Paul also learned the purpose of pain, by trial, long before Hobby Lobby painted it on faux barnwood. He writes, "And we know that in all things God works for the good of those who love him, who have been called according to his purpose" (Romans 8:28).

Now, this is encouraging, to be sure. But try saying these lines to someone who has just experienced something devastating: the loss of a child, a tornado destroying their neighborhood, losing life savings, being deployed into active combat—again. A verse like this might give you the heart tingles, but for other folks and for me at different points in my life, it churns us into angry psalmists, shaking fists into the air. Or into a disgruntled boxer, maybe Mike Tyson right before he bit off a chunk of Evander Holyfield's ear.

I am reminded of the character of Joseph in the Bible too. When you think of this biblical character, you might envision singing Broadway actors in marvelous rainbow coats, glittering lights, and encores. The truth of the matter is, Joseph lived a very traumatic life. His own brothers deceived and betrayed him. He was sold into slavery. He experienced all sorts of trials and sufferings. Yet, despite his struggles, Joseph, at the end of that round of trials in his life (there would surely be more), extended grace to his treacherous, then repentant brothers and said, "You intended to harm me, but God intended it for good . . ." (Genesis 50:20).

Joseph practiced forgiveness.

No matter where you are in your journey in life or recovery or both, perhaps you are also feeling the movement of how God is working in your circumstances and weaving something good from that something you thought was irredeemable. Maybe you can begin to see a break in the clouds.

Like Streetlamps

So, what bridges the gap between what God says about it (that pain can have a purpose) and how we can *feel* when things get hard? How can we move beyond this understanding into true forgiveness and radical compassion for what has hurt us?

Of course, there is research on the subject. My scientist husband says we try to make sense of our pain because we are human beings and want to understand and make sense of the world. Or how I see it: when it comes to trauma, science and spirituality do not have to be at odds. I love how Heather Kopp, author of *Sober Mercies*, puts it:

> My path in recovery and my path as a Christ follower didn't have to be in conflict. They could illumine and inform one another. Like streetlamps lining both sides of the street, they could light my way back to God.[28]

Research (and my own experience) shows that there are actions we can take. We can build protective factors like creating and sustaining safe, stable, nurturing relationships. We can heal our minds and bodies. We can see beyond the shadows to the light of good that Paul references in his letter to the Romans. We can move beyond mere sight or experience and allow this truth—the one where *all* things work for good—to transform us fully.

The Center for Disease Control and Prevention also suggests that raising awareness about trauma can work to change how people think about it. Bringing more into the light can work to swat away the mysterious places and darkness of pain. When we learn more about the causes of ACEs or AAEs, we can help to shift the focus from individual responsibility to community (and that includes faith-based community) solutions. We can reduce the stigma around seeking help for addiction or post-traumatic stress or other mental health challenges. We can promote nurturing, stable homes where children can flourish and are emboldened to use their voices—and where adverse experiences, like scaley (or feathery) dinosaurs, can be extinguished for good.

Here is a list of protective factors that can counter the effects of adverse childhood experiences and trauma and lead to our ability to forgive. These are ways that God has given us to walk alongside those struggling (and sometimes "those struggling" are *us*). As the author Manda Carpenter said, "We can't go back in time to fix our lowest, ugliest moments, but we can learn from them."[29]

Individual protective factors can include:

- Families that establish secure, steady, and supportive connections, ensuring children experience a dependable family environment that prioritizes their safety, well-being, and encouragement
- Healthy friendships and peer connections
- Sense of purpose
- Focus and prioritization of work and academics
- Healthy adults who serve as mentors or role models
- Positive interactions with and participation in community[30]

Now, before we continue on, maybe take a few moments to think about what protective factors are present in your life. If they are lacking, maybe it is time to ask God or friends and family (biological or chosen) to support you in building some. Building protective factors into your life may be your first step to seeing how God is moving. It may be your first step toward seeing purpose in the pain and forgiveness waiting on the horizon.

Chapter 7

When Healing Has Legs

To forgive is to set a prisoner free and discover that the prisoner was you.
—Lewis B. Smedes, *Forgive and Forget*

My addiction led me into more unsafe spaces than I can count. You've probably picked up on this by now. A couple of these places are scenes from a life that, looking back, doesn't feel like my own, but is. Sexual violence and trauma can do this: lead you to see things as if out of body. As a reminder, this is called *dissociation*. This type of trauma is also what has led me to places of forgiveness that shine brighter than any I've known. But it hasn't been an easy process, to forgive with abandon. To practice forgiveness and to pray radically for the heart to change, to let forgiveness in and resentment out.

I write about my experiences of sexual violence in other works, including my first book, *Downstairs Church*. What follows here is the second part of a chapter in that book that didn't make the cut—not because it wasn't important, but because I wasn't there yet. I wasn't ready to include what happened after the rape when I was fourteen years old and after years of hurt.

Here is the last part of the letter I wrote to the man who raped me:

Despite the pain and darkness and what I have lived through because of it, this is what I would say to you if I had the chance, the man who raped me when I was fourteen years old: I forgive you. While I couldn't see it at the time or for years after, I know now that you, too, came from a broken place and perhaps are still there. After all, we were both teenagers at that party drinking. We had our reasons for drinking so much, for wanting to escape. While I forgive (but never forget), my heart breaks for your broken place. I wear compassion like only someone who has experienced suffering can.

In this peaceful place of forgiveness, I'd also like to tell you there is something else there, a treasure in the sand. I can be grateful that I am a resilient woman who can get through anything with God's help. And importantly, I can also be grateful because I have been able to connect with the suffering of other women, women who have walked the road I have and far worse. And there are many of us. Too many. The resounding chorus of "me too" thunders around the globe.

Despite it all, now I can sing and truly mean that it is well with my soul.

Today, when I think about you, I am not angry. I am not resentful. Though I recognize it has taken me years to get to this place—and much support. It was never something I could do on my own, though I tried and tried. What I needed was a supernatural intervention. When I was able to realize this, when I was able to extend my hand to the One who was there with me lying in the snowbank, the One who walked through the years of self-destruction and addiction and hurt, the One who was there all along—when I was able to cry out and ask for my own forgiveness and love, something amazing and downright miraculous happened.

I was given a precious gift that I could then share with you.

Instead of hurt or anger, when I think of you, in my mind I see something like a Colorado mountain scene: awe-inspiring, purple-haze majesty covered in brilliant, shining snow. I think of God and how radical a life it is to follow Him. To forgive and love no matter what the cost. And sometimes it costs us dearly. I want to show you a glimpse of what this merciful God has given me. I want you to see and experience firsthand this incredible, unbelievable grace. This ridiculously persistent love. Today, I want to share my forgiveness with you and whisper gently as I extend my hands to yours that you are loved. There is purpose on the other side of your pain too.

The first time I shared these words in a blog article with *This Grit and Grace Life*, the editor called me and said she wanted to talk.[31]

This can't be good, I thought.

She was young and, I could tell, a bit nervous about the call.

As she started, I realized why she was nervous. She was about to give me guidance on how to talk about the forgiveness of the person who raped me.

"I think it's important for the reader to know that it didn't happen right away, that it's okay to forgive but not forget. We don't want to diminish anyone else's experience. Maybe there are women out there who aren't there yet and reading this might feel like they are wrong in being angry or wrong in how they feel toward their perpetrator."

I felt for her. Having this courageous conversation with a writer wasn't something they likely taught in Communications 101 or even 201.

"I get it," I said.

And I did get it. I knew that I did need to rework the article to speak to the woman not like me who had walked through healing to forgiveness, but to the woman who wasn't there yet. As writer and editor extraordinaire, Stephanie Duncan Smith says, "In sharing our stories, we need to make room for the reader."[32]

I shared about the supernatural intervention and how it took more than my own strength.

In my own strength, the last thing I'd ever do is forgive him.

Or *them*. If you are a woman like me, you know that there are usually more than one. The rape I experienced at the age of fourteen was just the beginning. Similarly, my own mother's struggles didn't end after a single event. Sexual violence and abuse were like termites boring into layers of our lives.

As Anne Lamott says, "Forgiveness is giving up all hope of having had a better past."[33] I'd like to add that it's not only giving up hope that things could have been different, dragging this monstrous thought around as the weight of it suffocates you. Forgiveness is reciprocal. Maybe before we are able to forgive others, we need to forgive ourselves first. Maybe we need to let go of the things we've done before turning toward the things done to us.

For me, these thoughts preceded the supernatural intervention, God swooping in to soften my heart and bring in empathy: prayer. For me, in any situation where forgiveness is an outcome, prayer is always part of the process.

When we are wrapped in forgiveness, God's love permeates. It conquers. It soothes.

There is an article originally called "I'm Still Learning to Forgive" from a 1970s edition of *Guideposts* by author and evangelist Corrie ten Boom. This woman was a Holocaust survivor and harborer of Jewish people in her family home during WWII. Her faith moved her to act justly and love graciously when everything around her shouted no.

No, don't stand up for what's right.

It will cost too much.

Corrie ten Boom, along with other family members, many who did not make it out of the concentration camps alive, chose to act in accordance with their beliefs, instead of being guided by fear. She then felt moved to share her own experience and hope with others, along with a message of forgiveness. During one of her talks at a church in Munich, Germany, in 1947, she saw a man she never expected to see again: a guard from the concentration camp where she and countless others endured unimaginable trauma.

In the article, she states:

And that's when I saw him, working his way forward against the others. One moment I saw the overcoat and the brown hat; the next, a blue uniform and a visored

cap with its skull and crossbones. It came back with a
rush: the huge room with its harsh overhead lights, the
pathetic pile of dresses and shoes in the center of the
floor, the shame of walking naked past this man. I
could see my sister's frail form ahead of me, ribs sharp
beneath the parchment skin.[34]

Corrie was faced with an opportunity to forgive—and
heal—that she wasn't prepared for. This man was a guard at
Ravensbrück. This moment did not wait for her to be ready.

The man looked at her and went on to describe that he had
become a Christian and asked for God's forgiveness. He
believed, now, that he was forgiven by God and a new cre-
ation. But he also knew at that moment that he wanted to ask
forgiveness from her too. Corrie went on to share:

And so woodenly, mechanically, I thrust my hand into
the one stretched out to me. And as I did, an incredible
thing took place ... For a long moment we grasped each
other's hands, the former guard and the former prisoner. I had never known God's love so intensely as I
did then.[35]

Practicing Forgiveness in Community

When I celebrated a year in recovery, I was flying high on a
pink cloud—like the amazing kind of shimmering clouds that
line a Floridian sunset sky. But then after my first sober birthday, a wave of new emotions hit me like an ocean liner during
a hurricane. I was suddenly confronted by all this messiness
and all this yuck and the pink soon disappeared. All these new

feelings bubbled up to the surface, and I had no idea what to do. And not just emotions, but the memories of the rape and other traumas too. Some I've shared with you here. And some I've spared your ears from hearing because, ultimately, this story is about you. In place of my story's particulars, our hope— my mother's and mine—is that you will see your own story in the context of the words we share.

> What are some of the feelings or emotions that are coming up for you? Can you recognize patterns in some of the same emotions you feel?

After nearly twenty years of burying the mess and the hurt and then having it resurface over the course of a year, it is no wonder that I didn't get carried out to sea then and there or instantly combust. Looking back now, I'm still not quite sure how I survived my first year of recovery or the few years after. What I do know is this: if I would have tried to do it alone, including forgive myself and others, there is no way that I could have.

I've learned that it is imperative to work through hard things in community, including past traumas. But you don't need to be in recovery from addiction like me to have this ring true.

Thankfully, during my first year sober, I connected with an outpatient treatment center that encouraged connection to others. I attended recovery meetings and sometimes forced myself to stay after closing prayer to talk with others. I had mentors and peers who walked alongside me and shared their experience, strength, and hope over coffee. I finally learned how to let other people into my life in an authentic (and sober) way for the first time.

Dealing with my own junk in recovery has not been the only "hard thing" that's happened. I wish that were true. I've experienced deaths of friends and family, horrible diagnoses, natural disasters, and last but not least, the global pandemic we've all dealt with. Things that my "worst-case scenario" thinking could not have dreamed up. The floor beneath me has shaken. Somedays it's shaking and when I look down, I'm standing over an abyss that is scary and dark. If I go back to my old, isolating ways when hard things happen—they will break me. The need for community never goes away.

The good news? When we are grounded in community and grounded in God in that community, we are able to withstand the storm. Suddenly over the abyss, a bridge appears that we can walk (or run) over. Your hands are holding it up. You hold me up. The recovery community and fellowship help us to see the path and walk ahead even when we aren't sure of what's ahead of us. We learn how to forgive the hard things together. We show each other how.

I'll never forget some of the things I've learned in meetings. People have shared with me all the hard things and all the beautiful things. I've heard how, through recovery, they were able to withstand the death of their spouse or child. The job lost. Home destroyed. Country ravaged. All the horrible things that in my mind I've secretly said, "If this happened to me, then maybe I would be justified in going back out. In using again. In going back to my old ways." And the good things too: the weddings, births, new friendships, and other lovely joys that shine like stars in the night.

In recovery, everything is supported. When hard things happen, or good things, my people are there to hold me up or cheer me on. Whatever life brings, I'm never alone. Living in community makes walking through the hard things, through all things—even forgiving people that are impossible to forgive—possible. It doesn't matter if you identify as being in recovery or not (though as I've said before, I think we are all in recovery from something). Whatever your hard thing is, community can bring healing and sustain it.

Choosing Healing

When we decide to begin a recovery journey, we choose healing. We can come to realize just how broken we are and how much support we need to make the kind of changes we want to make in our lives. We might begin to understand that transformation may cost us something (and not just the money we spend on outpatient treatment or recovery support services). If we are not willing to choose healing, then we are opting out, just like we might have spent years already in the active escape of our active addiction. Like hitting the small x on the screen to the right of the pop-up ad, every time we choose to walk away or turn our back on an underlying issue, it might disappear for a time, but it is likely going to resurface.

Choosing to heal and addressing our struggles is not something that we can do on our own. We cannot will ourselves by ourselves to heal. We can't choose healing by ourself and expect to make it out alive. Believe me, I've tried. We cannot lean in to our experiences of trauma to create new opportunities or forgive in radical ways unless we do this together.

Here, I'd like to encourage you with this truth again: you are not alone.

Just check out my newsletter (*Circle of Chairs* on Substack), and you'll see that there are thousands of folks like you who are on a healing journey. Sign up at https://CarolineBeidler.substack.com/.

There is a group of us, innumerable, like those beautiful shifting waves of black birds that create works of art in the sky as they flit here and there in perfect unison—we are all moving toward healing.

You may be like me and learned that reaching out for help is unsafe—or even impossible. It's no wonder that sometimes we think that we have to get through things on our own. Or that only we can help ourselves. This is simply not true. As human beings, we are made for connection. Allowing others into our experience can be scary, but it's such an important part of healing. One thing no one told me (and certainly not with their actions), but that I learned as I opened myself up to trusting others, is that it's okay to ask for help.

While this is true, it's also important to state that it's okay to be selective about who we share with. Once, in a small group during a college class, I blurted out that I was sexually assaulted as a freshman in high school and then again as an undergrad. The other women in the group just stared at me stunned, not knowing how to respond. I don't think any of them were familiar with the downstairs spaces of recovery communities where such transparency and vulnerability is the norm. I don't blame them. I may have overshared.

But we own our stories, and your story is yours to share whenever and however you need to.

But as you work through your traumas, it's a very empowering thing to be able to choose who to let into your life and who to be vulnerable with. Not everyone wants to talk about their experience on social media and that's okay. It's also important to consider that we don't have to ever go into the details of our trauma with everyone we meet. Trust me, you haven't heard the worst of my dirt. Connecting doesn't have to involve sharing explicit details of our stories or trauma with people we don't choose and who aren't safe or trusted people in our lives. We also need to be mindful about how the details of our stories can impact other people.

While you may want to share details and doing so can be incredibly healing, healing can also come from the simple acts of learning to trust and letting others love and care about us. When we experience the radical compassion of others, something incredible can begin to happen: we can start forgiving ourselves.

Transformation can occur gradually, like Southern winters, as we learn loving actions toward ourselves: practicing self-love and boundaries, learning to forgive, all within the loving space of community.

There are so many resources out there today that offer support too. Faith communities, counselors, physicians, treatment professionals, or recovery coaches are just a couple examples of people that can be there for you if you reach out. You can connect with my email community or storytelling platform, my private Facebook group: Downstairs Club (what happens in Downstairs Club stays in Downstairs Club), or reach out and I'll connect you with a person or organization in your local community who can help you find the support you need.

So how can we connect as people longing for connection but sometimes fearing it in a dreadful way, not trusting that it's real, that any connection exists *for real* outside the buzzword of community? Thanks to the internet and the experience of folks who have gone before us and found healing, there are so many ways. Sober activities through outpatient treatment centers, social media communities, support groups for trauma survivors, volunteer opportunities, and so much more! I love how poet Kate Baer puts it: "Pick up your heavy burdens and leave them at the gate. I will hold the door for you."[36]

When we can embrace our trauma histories, ours and our families before us—our whole stories—other signs of healing appear. We will be able to talk about the trauma without feeling upset or numb, function well in daily life (such as holding a job), treat ourselves in a safe and not self-destructive way, be in healthy relationships without feeling vulnerable or isolated. We will also be able to enjoy life, rely on ourselves and others, control overwhelming symptoms, and believe that we are worth it all.

Sound too good to be true? It's not.

I'm living proof that not only is healing possible, but forgiveness is, too.

Ultimately, recovery from trauma in all its forms is possible, and a huge part of this is realizing that we can cope in healthy ways and promote safety for ourselves and others. Protecting ourselves by setting healthy boundaries is one way to do this, and practicing forgiveness is another. It does not mean that we forget about the past. It does mean that it no longer holds such destructive power over our lives. As my mother once said to me, in her own way, and I say to my daughter and son: "You don't have to live my chains." You can know the freedom of forgiveness.

Five Actions You Can Take: Practice Forgiveness

- Write a letter to someone who you forgive (you don't have to mail it).
- Write a letter or poem to someone you are struggling to forgive (you can burn it).
- Commit to adding a new practice into your life, replacing unhealthy patterns with healthy ones (start going to a new social support or recovery group, watch a funny movie with friends, start a new hobby or job that ignites purpose).
- Catch your thoughts (when you start to focus on something or someone you might have resentment against, catch that thought and refocus on something lovely).
- Listen to someone else's story (at a recovery meeting, on a podcast, in a book).
- Finish this journal prompt:

  I feel radical compassion when . . .

Rhythm 3

Lean In to the Struggle—Everyday Courage

Chapter 8

On a Path to Change

After the shine wears off, the real spiritual work begins.
—Jen Hatmaker, *7: An Experimental Mutiny against Excess*

I'm glad I never got a purple butterfly tattoo on the small of my back. No offense to anyone else out there, but in my glory days, the term "tramp stamp" had not yet become common vernacular. If you have no idea what I am talking about, you are fortunate. There were a couple tattoos I toyed with over the years, looking up pictures and drawing elementary school sketches on my arms and thighs and ankles and back. Nabokov's butterfly (an airy bluish-purple), during my obsession with Russian literature (don't ask), or the Latin phrase "Per aspera ad astra" (through hardship to the stars) until I found out it was both a motto of Kansas and on the cardboard container of Pall Mall cigarettes. Neither stuck permanently (thankfully), but my fascination with butterflies remains.

Recovery, in the spiritual sense, can be a complete change. A *metamorphosis*. Did you know the concept of metamorphosis is way more complicated than we all learned about in fourth grade with the chart with clip art graphics of the egg, larva, pupa, and butterfly (long before YouTube, people)? The origin of the word itself comes from Greek roots: *meta* meaning change and *morphe* meaning form. Not until recently did I learn that there is no consensus among scientists and entomologists (bug-study people) for defining types of insect metamorphosis. There has been division internationally whether many of the species that do go through a process of metamorphosis should be given different names for different stages.[37]

I've encountered something similar in my work with women with co-occurring addiction and trauma, along with having dealt with this myself.

For many of us who seek addiction treatment, the topic of trauma is something that is not discussed for a long time—if ever—by mental health professionals in their approach to addiction. It took me a little over fifteen years of seeing innumerable therapists, counselors, psychiatrists, and addiction treatment specialists before (finally!) someone diagnosed me with post-traumatic stress disorder. It might be strange to hear this (unless you might need to hear it too), but as soon as those words were uttered in that therapist's office, a piece of me could finally relax. Not only did I have reasons for how I'd struggled so long, but I finally had hope that I could heal.

I had direction.

The sad reality is that many folks do not make the connection to trauma and therefore do not find direction. Maybe you are waiting too. Maybe you are on your own path to metamorphosis, yet no one is stepping in as you are moving from one stage of healing to the next to say, "Hey, you over there, larva or whatever, did you know that adding [fill in the blank] to your treatment will increase your sense of safety and agency and help to promote positive coping strategies?" Or perhaps a little less jargony: "Hey, you, have you experienced trauma and are not dealing with it? Do you need help learning how to address those symptoms?"

Many of us are waiting.

You are not alone. All of us need people to point out our blind spots when it comes to healing. We need someone like an entomologist for humans (a therapist, sponsor, mentor, friend) to guide us in the metamorphosis.

Your own presenting symptoms may not be post-traumatic stress, but if you have experienced trauma of any kind, you still may need to address how you are coping. It doesn't matter how long ago that thing (or those things) happened to you. Trauma symptoms can be debilitating and impact more than just our lives today.

In 2013, Facebook's chief operating officer Sheryl Sandberg wrote a bestseller called *Lean In: Women, Work, and the Will to Lead*. The contemporary definition of the phrase "lean in" is all about "grabbing opportunities without hesitation,"[38] whether that refers to opportunity for self-examination or opportunity for advancement professionally.[39]

The phrase has also been the subject of fierce criticism from feminists and scholars to social justice advocates, all the way to former First Ladies. And understandably. For many women, the idea of leaning into leadership roles or new opportunities or promotions places unrealistic emphasis on personal responsibility and opportunity. It sometimes fails, many would argue, to take into account women's real experience—particularly marginalized folks—of not being able to stand in (let alone lean in to) spaces of vulnerability or professional advancement.

While there are plenty of op-eds and tweets and social media posts about the irrelevance of the lean in concept, and while there may be some negative connotations with it, I'd like to suggest something a bit bold (I'm also practicing assertive communication).

Let's reclaim it.

As people who are choosing healing, let's reclaim it.

In water and snow sports, you can lean in to a wave, the wind, a slope, or a turn. You can lean in to a pitch, a throw, or a catch. I like to envision what the body does during a yoga sequence shifting through a sun salutation: moving, leaning, then right foot up, rising slowly, the momentum of arms like doors closing, opening, branches swaying in a storm to lift up knees on hinges, arms spread like wings. Leaning in and out. Flying.

And this is how I think we can choose to see it if we'd like to. When we say we are going to "lean in to the struggle," this can mean that we are going to face our struggles head on. We are not going to shrink back. We are not going to stay silent. We are not going to let shame swallow us. We are not going to let Monster have the last word. We are going to take heart.

We are going to lean in our bodies, minds, and spirits to the hard things and to community, not to stay in the struggle, but in order to heal.

The Best Friend Insurance Can Buy

My therapist's name was Lydia, and she was only a couple years older than me when we met. Even though she was relatively young, she had just been diagnosed with stage III breast cancer. She continued seeing clients even while undergoing extensive chemotherapy. She made me uncomfortable at first—selfishly so. I thought, *What the heck am I doing here? My problems are so small compared to yours right now.* It didn't make sense that I was the one in the chair needing help.

She was gracious (the way everyone I've ever met with cancer is), and she looked into my eyes, really listening. When her beautiful, curly strawberry blond hair started falling out and she replaced it with wild rainbow bobs or long, black Cher hair, it became more real what was happening. Lydia, as she confronted her sickness, sat across from me as I confronted mine.

I started having thoughts of using again, along with severe anxiety, including panic attacks, depression, and suicidal thoughts.

In other words, I knew I needed help. Again. Even though I thought I might have been in that butterfly stage of recovery, I was a larva.

I was a couple of years into recovery, about the same amount of time I had had before my last recurrence of use, so I knew this time that, if I wanted things to get better instead of worse, I had to reach out for help. I needed to find the everyday courage to lean in to change.

I described previously the triggering aspects of my internship at the veteran's hospital in the addiction treatment area. Those days as a "nontraditional student" are what ultimately led me to meet Lydia.

This is one of the first stories I told her:

On the first day of the internship in early September, I was a little flustered and a little sweaty, having had to bike about six miles from my little rented house downtown. The path was beautiful, along an inlet and through campus housing and the other towering buildings that made me feel like I was right where I needed to be.

But I wasn't prepared for what was going to happen next.

After some minor technology issues and not being able to get my badge printed and some other Advil-inducing situations, my supervisor (who happened to be the director of the treatment program) suggested I sit in on a therapy group called "acceptance and commitment therapy."

"Sure!" I exclaimed merrily (but not with too much excitement, as I wanted to appear "put together" and "professional"), then bopped into the group room and closed the door behind me.

They had already started, and everyone looked up as I entered and then accidentally swung my large, black North Face backpack into an amputee.

"Excuse me, sir, I'm so sorry."

Not a great start.

He just stared at me, and I wasn't sure if it was my hair (it was dyed black at this time) or my choice of clothing (conservative chic on a Goodwill budget), but he rolled his eyes. I looked toward the group facilitators, two imposing men who towered above everyone, who both nodded and pointed with their eyes, then chins, to the only empty chair in the circle right between two older men.

I squeezed into my place and had to bring both of my shoulders into a little shrug to not touch the men on either side of me who looked a little too familiar with things I could never possibly know about. The room smelled like moldy apartment and Marlboros and Mountain Dew and flat coffee with two packets of sugar substitute. My naive excitement blew up like a roadside bomb and was replaced by the realization that I was in over my head.

These were men of varying ages who had served in Vietnam and Iraq and Iran and Africa and Germany and Japan. All had seen active combat. The facilitators dove into exercises from the manual that I would become familiar with by the end of the year. I heard pieces of the information, and, with a pen and notebook, took a note here and a note there—the only one in the room doing so.

It was time for a practice exercise, and I was thankful to be able to stand up and breathe the air around me more fully. I was paired with the only other woman (the other one had left), and everyone was told to put our chairs together, touch the tips of our knees, and make eye contact. The purpose of the exercise was to get vulnerable with another human being.

Easy enough, I thought, along with, *I'm really glad there is another woman in here.*

Little did I know how difficult this exercise was going to be. How ill-prepared I was for letting myself be seen and for allowing myself to *feel*.

The woman had kind eyes and mousy brown, unwashed hair and super-defined biceps. She smiled at me as we sat down and pushed our chairs closer until our knees kissed, and we started the long gaze. A second, then two, then ten, and we both started shifting in our seats. I could feel the rough upholstery on my elbows. I looked down for a moment and noticed all the stains in the carpeting. We made eye contact again, and I remembered the sign on the door when I approached the building not even an hour before, asking that no firearms be brought into the building.

"We've only had a couple incidents," my internship supervisor assured me. But right then, my mind (an imaginative one at that) started to go wild with all the possible scenarios of the "incidents."

Focus.

I looked more intentionally into her eyes, and in an instant, it felt like I was hit in the gut by someone with knuckle rings. There was something—a sadness, a familiarity—that struck me. Her soft brown eyes spoke something to me in a language that I understood. I could feel the tears welling. Then, her tears started dropping down her cheeks too.

The two therapists in the room were looking at me; or maybe they weren't, but it felt like it.

How was I ever going to do this, work with people in addiction who had experienced trauma, if this first exercise led me to fall apart?

After a couple more minutes that felt like years, it was all over. The woman and I silently moved back to our chairs and sat down. She got out her phone and stared at it, and I looked down at my notebook.

What the Heck Just Happened?

After a couple of weeks, I realized that as I was learning this model of group therapy, I was going through it myself. But my professional boundaries crumbled under the weight of being triggered. The men. The smells. The lack of safety I felt (all in my mind, yet it felt so tangible). On several occasions, I ran out of the room with panic or vomit welling in my throat.

The feedback I got from my supervisor was that the staff were "concerned" about my performance. The flat affect (or no emotion) on my face. My silence during staff meetings. My inability to connect with the clients in a one-on-one setting. I had to give some explanation, so I alluded to my own past with addiction and trauma, how I knew this was going to be challenging for me and how I thought I'd be up for the challenge.

I didn't know that it was going to derail me.

Having recounted this to Lydia in a therapy session many seasons later, she agreed that my trauma history was being triggered and that it was very important to address it.

"A lot of times," she said, "after a couple of years sober, after quitting the alcohol, drugs, or other numbing agents, these things start to come up: tough things that have been buried."

I knew that early recovery sometimes brought emotions like that of a preteen (including the ridiculous crushes), but I didn't realize that other stuff was going to come bubbling up to the surface like fluorescent fish near a nuclear plant. Lydia suggested I go through an evidence-based treatment called Seeking Safety.[40] This therapy model is one of the only ones that research has shown to be effective in treating co-occurring trauma and addiction in a one-on-one or group therapy setting. It focuses on how to promote safety in relationships and offers thinking and actions centered around building healthy coping skills. This pathway became another of many to lead me on a recovery and healing journey.

This treatment appealed to me because, as she described it, it was well structured (and how I love structure), and I knew I needed to try something different. I was ready to not only lean in to the work but lean in to the solution, lean in to something new. All I could do was nod my head in agreement as she went over the twenty-five topics that the workbook covered:

- Safety
- Taking Good Care of Yourself
- Honesty
- Asking for Help
- Recovery Thinking
- Setting Boundaries in Relationships
- Healthy Relationships
- Creating Meaning
- Compassion
- Detaching from Emotional Pain (Grounding)
- Community Resources
- Discovery
- Getting Others to Support Your Recovery
- Integrating the Split Self
- Commitment
- Respecting Your Time
- Coping with Triggers
- Self-Nurturing
- Red and Green Flags
- Life Choices

Yes, yes, and more yes. I nodded my head and told Lydia yes—I wanted to work on all those things. I was tired of living like a victim, tired of the lingering effects of trauma like fear

ON A PATH TO CHANGE   113

and disordered eating and unhealthy relationships and boundary issues and all of it. I wanted to learn more about how I could step up and take action, be bold, and have courage. I wanted to lean in to the struggle instead of run from it.

> Have you had triggering experiences show themselves in your own life? Things that threaten to derail you or attack your sense of safety and peace? And importantly, have you found coping strategies that can help? Maybe it's time that you consider reaching out for more support?

Lydia was one person who helped me see that issues were lurking under the surface, even in early recovery. My trauma was crouching and waiting for me. And I had two choices. You do too. We can run (e.g., drink, use, eat, cheat, escape, [fill in the blank]), *or*, we can face our hard things with courage and lean in to the support and treatment options we can find.*

Here I'd like to pause and mention a couple other evidence-based treatment options for trauma recovery. I want to make sure that one of the things this book *doesn't* do is lead you to believe that your healing is something that only you are responsible for. That you have to do it alone: a "pull yourself up by your bootstraps" sort of fallacy. There are tools. There are different resources. There is a myriad of pathways to help us heal from trauma.

---

* Over the next year and during the rest of my graduate program, I worked with Lydia. God took me through the Seeking Safety treatment and led me to grow through some of the most intense triggers I had in my early recovery. I believe therapy and God can work together. While we rest in our larva (or maybe pupa) stage, something is being worked out for our good. Something mysterious and powerful and purposeful.

- Seeking Safety: as mentioned earlier, this is one of the only evidence-based treatment models for co-occurring substance use disorder and trauma treatment.[41]
- Trauma-focused psychotherapies: EMDR (eye movement desensitization and reprocessing), CBT (cognitive and behavioral therapy), and certain types of exposure therapy like PE (prolonged exposure) are found to be helpful, especially for individuals with post-traumatic stress disorder or PTSD. These types of interventions require trained and licensed mental health professionals.[42]
- Creating trusting relationships: research shows that creating healthy and secure attachments of relationships with others, including therapists, can help you heal more quickly and in more lasting ways.[43]
- Medications or pharmacological treatment: for many individuals (I'm raising my hand), medications for the treatment of depression, anxiety, PTSD, and more can help for short-term or long-term treatment of trauma symptoms and related mental well-being symptoms.[44]
- Trauma-informed peer support: author, activist, and founder of the Center for Courage and Renewal, Parker Palmer, wrote, "When you speak to me about your deepest question, you do not want to be fixed or saved; you want to be seen and heard, to have your truth acknowledged and honored." Peer support opens up the opportunity to be seen and heard and have our experiences validated. There is immeasurable power in this simple phrase: "me too."[45]

There are many excellent resources out there that talk more in-depth about these different options for treatment. My recommendation to you is to learn more about what is available. Talk to trusted friends, family, or other supports. Then start making decisions about the next steps for your healing journey or that of a loved one.

Chapter 9

The Roots of Family Trauma

Her sponsor told her once that the only love she knows what to do with is the kind of love that breaks a person over and over again.

—Gabriela Garcia, *Of Women and Salt*

Being an author and recovery advocate working with people all over the world, I probably don't have to tell you the kinds of weird and sometimes argumentative messages and emails I get from time to time. I've learned that if something looks like it was sent by an internet troll, it likely was. All this being said, what made me pause recently was this:

"What about the men?"

Now, as is my style (hopefully you've noticed this by now), I'm going to be real with you. When I first saw the question posed by some random guy who found my website, I retorted back by saying, "What about them?"

I'm not always here to speak to or encourage every person. My calling feels more directed to women and folks who have had experiences that are quite common among women and need their own special attention. But after I did a reality check with my husband (whenever I get weird or suggestive or any type of message that makes me uncomfortable, I tell him first), I started asking myself the same question.

"What about the men? Is it possible that we all experience the impact of family trauma, unhealthy patterns, and the need to disrupt them?"

Not long after this unsettling question where I was encouraged to do some deep reflection, I received a story submission to my blog *Circle of Chairs* that I published in my weekly newsletter.[46]

In the submission, a man named Jason shares his journey of overcoming addiction and trauma, highlighting his upbringing rooted in chaos from family trauma and sexual abuse. He bravely details his descent into self-destructive behavior, including addiction and failed relationships.

While his story is tough to read, like many of our stories, and even tougher to have lived through, Jason finds redemption through recovery. Through the support of different pathways of recovery, he experiences personal growth, forgiveness, and spiritual awakening, leading him to ultimately embrace and lean into a new life.

"I found God a year into my program, and it was unexpected! The principles of the Twelve Steps had already begun to change me. I didn't expect to have a spiritual awakening."

Jason's story is one of resilience and transformation. He didn't expect to have a spiritual awakening, but he did. His story is also an important example of how anyone—*anyone*—can struggle with family trauma and ultimately heal. Jason's own experience of family trauma, including sexual abuse, led him down a harrowing path and one that threatened the root of his life. Yet change happened.

In the field of forest pathology, there is an interesting observed phenomenon that involves root diseases of trees. Diseases begin in the roots or lower area of the tree and oftentimes cause decaying wood to kill the tree.[47] For most trees, root diseases can be the deadliest. A specific type of root disease is called the black stain root disease, which is carried by certain types of beetles or weevils. According to the US Forest Service, this disease is especially treacherous for Douglas firs, and it not only impacts the growth of individual trees, but it can spread to close, neighboring trees as well.[48]

In Jason's story, it is clear how something like a root disease threatened to take hold of his life and choke out the light. His early years were overwhelmed by adverse experiences and trauma. His life could have (understandably) never recovered from them. He could have stayed isolated, resentful, untrusting, and steeped in addiction. Who could blame him? His own trauma could impact his children and others' children. Yet he worked to heal. And heal he has—and does daily.

> You may have your own "root diseases" that may have threatened your well-being or are threatening your well-being right now. What are they? Take some time to think about how early experiences in your life, or in the lives of family members, may impact your recovery today.

Deep in the soil, below the surface, there can exist a lineage of trauma. Jason hints at challenges with his own family. Perhaps the perpetrator of his abuse, as is most often the case, was a victim too. Perhaps members of his family turned to alcohol or other drugs to cope with the *dis*-ease of life. My mother and I have shared pieces of our own family's connection to trauma too. Rachel Marie Kang in *The Matter of Little Losses* shares, "We inherit injury through our bloodline. We carry the ache of our earliest ancestors, wearing life's first loss like it is some kind of skin."[49]

After reading Jason's story for the first time, perhaps you can relate to what I was feeling after reading it for the first time too. His is a gritty journey. One that begins with really tough things and ends on the other side where there is hope and recovery. Jason's faith, too, inspires. In the same way that addiction doesn't discriminate, trauma doesn't either. Yet, Jason leans in to the tough parts of his story to heal.

Jason shares, "I didn't expect to have a spiritual awakening. The thing is that when you work the steps and really apply the principles of the program to your daily life, it changes you from the insides out. It cleans out the conduit between you and God."

Sometimes what happens to us and to our families, the hardships we endure, indeed the trauma too, all of it can have a purpose, a meaning. I've experienced it in my own life and witnessed this in the lives of women I've worked with or spoken to over the years. The men too. No matter what gender you identify with, trauma is universal, as is the need to find coping strategies to deal. Our trauma is only the beginning of our stories. When we look at and lean into the root of our issues, we can begin to heal.

Historically Speaking

I've heard people talk about "roots" in recovery meetings. Part of doing what Alcoholics Anonymous calls the fourth step* is

---

* *Make a searching and fearless moral inventory of ourselves.*

knowing that to heal, we need to get to the root of our problem with substances. To make a searching and fearless moral inventory of ourselves is to examine what the underlying causes are, dig deep beneath the surface, and expose what is hidden underground. A "root" is:

> that part of a vascular plant normally underground. Its primary functions are anchorage of the plant, absorption of water and dissolved minerals and conduction of these to the stem, and storage of reserve foods. The root differs from the stem mainly by lacking leaf scars and buds, having a root cap, and having branches that originate from internal tissue rather than from buds.[50]

It is interesting to note that roots are similar to the branches of a tree or plant in many ways. The difference, as the encyclopedia states, is that these branches "originate from internal tissue rather than from buds."

So, what is the root of something we're recovering from, and if it's intergenerational trauma, what is the root that caused it?

Intergenerational Trauma in the Modern World

Many people write about and point to the Holocaust as an extreme example of human suffering and loss. With good reason—it was. The United States Holocaust Memorial Museum shares that genocide is "a coordinated plan of different actions aiming at the destruction of essential foundations of the life of national groups, with the aim of annihilating the groups themselves." This is horrifying on innumerable levels.

There are other horrific examples of mass suffering and killing like the Rwandan Massacre (1994), Armenian Genocide (1915–1916), Khmer Rouge Killing Fields in Cambodia (1976–1978), the Great Purge and the Ukrainian Famine during Stalin's Communist regime (1929–1953), and mass killings during Mao Zedong's regime (1949–1959). With others, like the California genocide of the mid-late 1800s (where over 80 percent of indigenous peoples in the area were killed), or the 1921 Tulsa Race Massacre, little of which has become common knowledge or been taught in most history classes.

Or, more recent examples like Sudan, Haiti, Ukraine, Palestine, Israel. This list, tragically goes on.

For many who are BIPOC (Black, indigenous, people of color), historical trauma has led to intergenerational trauma too. Dr. Kyaien O. Conner, a licensed social worker and associate professor in the Department of Mental Health Law and Policy at the University of South Florida, researches behavioral health disparities in racial and ethnic minority communities.

In an article for *Psychology Today*, Dr. Conner states that:

> Slavery, the Civil War, Jim Crow, and Segregation are all examples of historical traumas. Each individual event was profoundly traumatic and when you look at these events as a whole, they represent a history of sustained community disturbance and devastation. Black Americans are a resilient people, but these historical traumas have lasting consequences for individuals, families, and communities.

She goes on to state that:

[. . .] unfortunately, for Black Americans, historical traumas are not just in the past. They are playing out for us
daily, triggering emotional and physiological responses
that can be impossible to control and extremely difficult
to cope with. In the Black community, individuals not
only carry the burden of historical trauma, but must
also navigate daily race-based stressors including dis-
crimination, oppression and microaggressions.[51]

There are those traumas that many of us can relate to, and
then there are some like the experiences of Black Americans
that women like me, though having experienced my own
shades of trauma, will never know because of privilege as a
white woman. I believe this is important to state here because
of my limitations to talk about historical and intergenerational
trauma for every person, every woman. I will never be able to
do this and do it justice, yet a conversation about intergenerational trauma would be incomplete if I do not say something.

What does this bring up for you? Can you relate to the
experiences of genocide survivors, BIPOC individuals, and
other under-resourced, marginalized folks? Can you relate to
Jason's story or perhaps mine?

Has your mother experienced the same type of trauma you
have? Has she endured years of unhealthy relationships, inef-
fective coping strategies, or quiet, lonely struggles?

Or maybe your family tree has these branches: divorce, military trauma, poverty, emotional neglect, verbal or sexual abuse?

Wherever you find yourself in this conversation, I trust
that you are right where you need to be as you are reading

these words. I know I am, in the writing of them. Right now, dear reader, I wish we could take a long, deep breath together.

Angela Yvonne Davis, American author and activist, says this: "I am no longer accepting the things I cannot change. I am changing the things I cannot accept."

Regardless of our identities or the specifics of our suffering (as important as these things are), the consequences of trauma for those who survive and their descendants can be catastrophic, becoming the bones and blood of the survivors—the very makeup of our DNA. Roots that lead to the visible tree above ground growing. If you consider the way roots move like veins through the body, inextricably linked, we can feel how our collective experiences are connected, even if in a minuscule way.

What is so powerful in the me-too of looking at our trauma experiences in light of what others experience or have experienced?

I'd like to argue that freedom—a supernatural freedom—can come when we recognize that we are sharing in the larger suffering of the world. We can lean in to our individual struggle, and we can lean in to our collective struggle. When we experience trauma or suffering that our families or other folks in the human family have experienced, we are sharing in the hard, beautiful truth of what it means to be human and what it means to work toward healing. Together. Even when what we experience is different. Even if we will never know the pain of someone else's story. We can all relate to the tremor of trauma: this world's trouble.

Chapter 10

Tear Down to Build Up

Without somehow destroying me in the process, how could God reveal himself in a way that would leave no room for doubt? If there were no room for doubt, there would be no room for me.

—Frederick Buechner, *The Alphabet of Grace*

My friend Nadine kept asking me if I wanted to join her wellness accountability group through a fitness program called BODi where she was a lead coach. This was a hard no from me for months. Maybe even a year. No time. No money. No interest. No stamina. Where and how and on what planet could I fit *one more thing* into my overflowing schedule?

Have a group of women I don't know hold me accountable for working out and eating healthy?

I think not.

Eventually, as happens with strong and healthy women who try to support me, she wore me down. Her latest offer, "Will you join me for an eight-week weight lifting program?" was enticing.

I'd read about how lifting weights in your forties helps with a whole host of things like bone density loss, sagging skin, and a limping metabolism. It was reasonably affordable too, but I did what I do (usually) when I want to spend money over a certain amount: I asked the hubs.

He was hesitant at first, like most good money managers are, but then suggested I try it if I wanted to.

"We'll be supporting Nadine's goals too, right?"

Yes, my husband, along with being a great steward of our finances, is also very kind.

"Yes, I can set some fitness goals, and we can support Nadine's side hustle."

It was a win-win.

Little did I know, in eight short weeks, that I'd come to love my morning workouts, one of the BODi super-trainers named Joel Freeman, and the rest of the lifters in a rainbow of leathery-metallic stretchy pants and sports bras on the screens behind him.[52] I'd also learn about some of the benefits of weight lifting like burning fat, losing weight, and seeing my ab muscles (sort of) for the first time. Something that, especially after a twin pregnancy, I thought would never happen. I'd even learn how I could still burn calories, praise Jesus, even hours after each workout. This is called the "after-burn" effect.

The program consisted of workouts five days per week for about forty-five minutes a day that included weight lifting, HIIT (high intensity interval training), and core. In other words, a shock to my system.

The first week I couldn't walk. I limped around the house like I'd just run a marathon or got stuck in a drain pipe. By the second and third weeks, something started happening.

A physical trainer says that "when you strength train, you tear muscle fibers, but that is part of the growing process." This same trainer goes on to say, "You shouldn't lift the same muscle group every day because the muscle needs to heal in order to rebuild."[53]

This process, while confusing in some respects, rang true. In order to grow, I needed to first experience a ripping apart. Tearing down.

There is something about the triumph story in sports that makes me want to jump up and cheer. Part of why I became so attached to the LIIFT MORE program with BODi (formerly Beachbody) was because of Joel Freeman's story.

Now, looking at him, you might not think that this tattooed Texan has experienced any adversity other than missing a spot of suntan oil before hitting an LA pool party. But the more I learned about his story and how he rose through the ranks as if by chance, by showing up and saying yes, the more I liked him. He worked hard, first as a trainer at a gym franchise and then making connections with just the right folks at just the right time. Joel motivates others to not only get healthy but be realistic about it. For instance, he often shares that it's okay to be disciplined with your diet and also eat a cheeseburger every once in a while. My kind of trainer.

I've had weeks upon weeks of his online programs through BODi and spent hours with my very own funny and motivating personal trainer—and joking questions from my husband: "Are you spending too much time with Joel?" Training for my physical health reminds me that getting well physically involves more than just sitting around and willing my twin skin (twin and multiples moms know what I'm talking about) to melt away. I can't just pray my way to a lifted booty.

The same is true for mental and spiritual health. I've learned there are actions we can take every day that will improve our spiritual fitness over time.

What you've lived through and what your ancestors lived through does not have to be forever written into your genetic code and passed down to your children. This is a bold statement, and it's true.

When I think about what my mother lived through, I am overcome with emotion. Both sorrow and joy. I think about what she has survived (some in this book), and I both shudder and am in awe of her—and so many of us like her who have lived through hard things.

As Glennon Doyle famously said (and titled her podcast), "We can do hard things."[54]

But how?

How can we move from a place of profound hurt and healing to one of courage? How can we move beyond those branches dripping with memory and ache and the hard stuff of life toward healing?

How can we lean in to the struggle with courage?

Let's move beyond story into action. I'd like to talk about some practical tools and tips. How can we let the stories form in us something new and beautiful and bold and healing?

Two words:

Spiritual formation*

---

* If you are completely put off by any mention of "spiritual formation," because it sounds churchy, first off, thank you for continuing to read. I feel you. And I've been there. Can I encourage you to keep reading—and keep listening with an open mind? I'd also love to hear your story. Send a message by connecting with the QR code at the back of the book.

A Closer Walk

Dallas Willard says spiritual formation is the process of:

> transformation of the inmost dimension of the human being, the heart, which is the same as the spirit or will. It is being formed (really, transformed) in such a way that its natural expression comes to be the deeds of Christ done in the power of Christ.[55]

What does spiritual formation have to do with healing from intergenerational or family trauma? And what can we do with any of this if we are something other than Christian?

Regardless of the path you are on in life or recovery (or whether you identify with the concept of spiritual formation or not), there are practical action steps that you can take that can move you (as they have moved me) toward disrupting unhealthy patterns and finding healing.[*,56] Let's start with one of my favorites.

Read

Reading is still cool, people. And helpful for spiritual formation. Can we turn off the television and tune in to the archaic sound of pages turning or maybe an audiobook? Books by other sojourners about their recovery, trauma healing, or faith walk can be helpful. In my own life, I've learned so much from modern giants of the faith. In scripture, yes, but also those I find in my local bookstore.

---

* Much of this section was originally published with the Grit and Grace Project.

Here is an oldie but goodie: *Anything: The Prayer That Unlocked My God and My Soul*. In this book, Jennie Allen talks about how someone else's words, Katie Davis's in particular (the author of *Kisses from Katie*), inspired her to take bold action and turn to God with a new prayer that ultimately changed her life. One of my latest favorites that inspires boldness and courage is *Gutsy* by Natalie Franke. I love it. Reading books from other pilgrims on the path paired with reading the Bible can be an incredible combination for spiritual formation.

Pray

Prayer is an accessible tool for spiritual formation that can be done anywhere. My favorite time to pray? When I'm walking my dog.

I love how John Throop from Trinity Episcopal Church in Portsmouth, Virginia, describes prayer:

> Prayer can be offered in silence and in reflection on God's Word. We can pray through the singing of psalms, hymns, and spiritual songs. As Augustine, bishop of Hippo, said in the fourth century, "He who sings prays twice." We can use The Book of Common Prayer or other sacred texts available for worship and private prayer. We might want to employ a pattern for prayer. A familiar approach is the ACTS method: Adoration, Confession, Thanksgiving, and Sanctification.[57]

Or as my pastor recently put it: "Good prayer—and a right relationship with God—requires both words and silence."

Find the type of prayer or meditation that works for you. Whether that is an early morning cup of coffee and quiet time or a jog with a power greater than you, as some of my recovery friends like to say. Just like there are multiple pathways of recovery, there are innumerable ways to connect with the spiritual.

Get Vulnerable

Some circles might call this confession. I like to refer to this pouring forth of ourselves—including hurts, wrongs, and muck—as vulnerability. When we can be radically vulnerable and honest, we receive the gift of radical healing.

Madeleine L'Engle in *Walking on Water: Reflections on Faith and Art* says, "When we were children, we used to think that when we were grown-up, we would no longer be vulnerable. But to grow up is to accept vulnerability. [. . .] To be alive is to be vulnerable."[58]

Repentance (vulnerability that requires a turn or change of action) is a heart action that takes this all a bit deeper. It is confessing with our feet. Eugene Peterson, in his awesome book that I'm praying makes a comeback called *A Long Obedience in the Same Direction: Discipleship in an Instant Society*, says that "the usual biblical word describing the way that we say no to the world's lies and the yes we say to God's truth is *repentance*." He goes on to state, "Repentance is not an emotion. It is not feeling sorry for your sins. It is a decision. It is deciding that you have been wrong in supposing that you could manage your own life. . . ."[59]

I love this idea of repentance as an action, moving beyond the mind or even heart. In the same way, vulnerability is something we do, not feel. When we can be real with each other about our hurts and hang-ups, transformation happens.

Connect in Community

All these ideas for modern spiritual formation (that aren't so modern), can be done in the quiet of solitude. They can also be practiced in community. We can read reflectively with others in a small group or Bible study. We can pray with our friends or family or in a church service. We can even share vulnerably with others and confess our struggles with each other. As those of us in addiction recovery know too, community not only holds us accountable but can help us to identify those areas where shame is holding us back.

In fellowship with each other, there is life. When we open ourselves to the power of community, we open ourselves up to receive a gift. When we tell each other our deep and murky secrets, when we let others into our dark, muddy pools of ick, something miraculous happens: we slowly open a door to healing. And if we don't—well, if we don't, we can stay stuck. Or worse.

Laura McKowen in *We Are the Luckiest*, a memoir about her own struggle with alcoholism, says, "One stranger who understands your experience exactly will do for you what hundreds of close friends and family who don't understand cannot. It is the necessary palliative for the pain of stretching into change. It is the cool glass of water in hell."[60]

The strength and beauty and "cool glasses of water" that fellowship and community bring is one of the most incredible gifts of recovery.

Rest

It's easy to get going a million miles per hour and not slow down. After all, there is no shortage of *stuff to do* in today's world. But it is a priority, even in scripture (and for all mental health practitioners and counselors), that we rest. Especially in the Western world where productivity is for many of us a golden calf (Exodus 32:1–4).

Similar to how we need to schedule rest days when weight training so that our muscles can heal, we need time for our bodies, minds, and spirits to renew. One of my favorite ways to do this: the weekend nap. If my kids are resting or watching a movie, I grab a book and my favorite plush purple blanket and doze. I also take off workout days. I schedule in time when I am not looking at my phone or answering emails. I sit down without anything to distract me. As my Instagram friend and author Manda Carpenter puts it, I allow myself to get bored.

Spiritual formation is a process, a pilgrimage, a journey without a destination. The journey itself is the point.[61] While our stories and histories bring challenges and struggles, we can also dig into the past, learn from those who are walking ahead of us, and commit to taking courageous action toward healing.

Chapter 11

Whiffs of Grace

Your brokenness will turn to wholeness.

—Timothy Willard

Heather Kopp has been in publishing for decades, starting out as a columnist and then going on to edit and write over two dozen nonfiction books. Her recovery memoir, *Sober Mercies: How Love Caught Up with a Christian Drunk*, tells her story of anguish, then redemption, and a cycle of addiction that God miraculously and mercifully breaks. Not only in her own life, but in her son Noah's as well.

Heather speaks of the shame surrounding addiction for women, especially Christian women, and how challenging it was for her, during her struggle with alcohol, to move through the sticky religious notion that addiction is somehow a moral failing.

"I was taught that alcohol was a sin issue only. And so, while drinking I function like I need to try harder, I need to read my Bible more, I need to keep trying and trying and trying. But no matter how hard I tried I could not get a handle on this."[62]

You might be able to relate.

Even if alcohol is not your thing, there is likely something that you can't get a handle on or haven't been able to control in the past. A cycle of need or want or obsession that pulls you away from the holy and toward the temporal, bodily, ash.

Each page of *Sober Mercies* brought me closer to her story, and closer to my own.

Heather hid travel bottles of wine in boots and secretly drank them in restaurant bathroom stalls. I feel the icy stillness of a marriage on the brink. I smell the stale bittersweet of red stains on the floor. I relate so much with her confusion and constant questioning: why—if she didn't want to drink—did she keep on doing it?

Heather married young, and it wasn't until after her divorce in her late twenties that she was enticed by alcohol.

Her belief that "as a good Christian, you don't drink" faded in the background, and soon she was even disillusioned by parts of her faith.

In her new marriage, the old belief system gave way to a new one: drinking is what sophisticated people do. But soon, her normal, classy wine sipping plummeted messily into unmanageability. The phenomenon of craving took over, what some in recovery circles call the "cunning, baffling, and powerful" allure of substances.

What compounded the shame surrounding her drinking was her job in Christian publishing. By day, she was writing and editing books about prayer and relationships, and by night, stealing away to sneak alcohol when she could. No matter how much she tried to stop by white-knuckling her way through a whole day without alcohol, she couldn't.

Around this time, her son Noah also began struggling with addiction. The family even hosted an intervention to address Noah's alcohol and drug use, all while Heather hid her drinking (or so she thought) with the same expert precision that she edited a manuscript.

At forty-three years old, the pain was unbearable.

This is when she encountered God in a new way. Finally, a moment of surrender that led her into treatment.

"It felt like I wouldn't have made it across the line if God hadn't met me halfway and dragged me over."

God showing up during this moment of surrender was also one of the many miracles she experienced on her addiction recovery journey. According to Heather, there was no other way to explain such a sudden laying down of all the burdens she had been carrying—and a beautiful picking up of the peace that only God provides.

Heather says that her surrender moment came as "a combination of [her] willingness meeting up with God's mercy."[63]

Enough to Know that He Is Love

Have you been here, reader? Maybe in trying some of the practical suggestions and tools I mentioned earlier, you yourself have been inching toward freedom? Maybe you are beginning to understand what it feels like to lay it down (whatever your "it" is) and pick up something new, something lighter. Maybe you are, like Heather, ready to lean in to the struggle and practice courage every day because the need was born out of tragic necessity (more on this in a minute). Or perhaps, like me or my mother, you've had things happen a long time ago that have too long held your present and future hostage.

After reading *Sober Mercies*, I decided to do what many of us folk in recovery do: I reached out. To Heather. I found her email on her website and thanked her for her words. I told her how they impacted me and then asked if she might want to connect. I never expected she'd say yes.

She said yes.

And then maybe.

She asked if I'd read her blog. I said no.

I could almost feel the silent pause over email.

Heather then expressed concern that after reading it, I might have second thoughts. My interest was piqued and I grabbed my laptop.

What I discovered was horrible and tragic. With intentional detail, she wrote about the events that happened a couple years after her memoir was published. Doing more research, I discovered the truth and why Heather was unsure about connecting.

This is an excerpt of my response email back:

"I felt a tugging to reach out, not really expecting a response but hoping for one. I've been so touched by your book. And now, after reading through some of your blog posts tonight, I am speechless. There are no words, only my heart listening. I cannot imagine the grief and pain that you have experienced over the last couple of years."

I knew, after getting to know more of Heather's story, that hers is a perfect picture of the movement of God's story throughout all our lives: redemptive—again and again and again. Relentless. No matter what. Even in the struggle, the trauma, the REALLY hard things.

Heather agreed to an interview with me. The first since the shooting when her son Noah shot and killed three people and then was gunned down by police in Colorado Springs. Noah's own mental health challenges, addiction, and any possible motive for the crime, a horrific puzzle to everyone, including Heather.

When we spoke, Heather shared about the tragedy. The mental anguish and breakdown she experienced following it. A recurrence of substance use and the desire to numb and melt away. She told me how she felt deserted by the God she had followed—and written about—all her life. How she felt betrayed. How she questioned the very existence of a Father that could take her firstborn son and stand by as he committed such atrocities.

And then she told me about how women in recovery surrounded her. About how God showed up in unexpected places: in the open arms and soft smiles of familiar strangers, in ragtag circles smelling of stale coffee in church basements. And ultimately, she related how God spoke a word to her one Sunday morning while taking communion:

"I heard God saying to me, this terrible thing happened, but what if in that darkest moment, you were still held by love? Can it be enough to know that I love you and that I am love and you are held in that love no matter what happens? And I said to God: 'Yes.'"

Heather's story reminds us that no matter what trauma happens in our past or present, we are all connected by these shared experiences of humanity. And what is more, we have a choice in how we respond. We can give in to the trauma and tragedy—some of which can strike even after we find recovery—or we can trudge on, leaning in to healing. We can use the tools we've been given, like practicing courage, to step out of the darkness and into a new day.

Heather's story and others like it have helped me look at my own experience with a touch more grace and compassion. A bit more freedom. We don't have to pretend to forget or pretend to understand why trauma happens, but we can be present for what comes next, no matter what it is.

Cut Off the Branch

Coffee, a farmers' market, and a slow brunch with our friends, Julie and Charles, provide a prolonged exhale. My husband and I like to schedule these morning dates when we have the energy. Parents of little ones, know what I mean?

During a recent meal, we went from casual conversation to digging a bit deeper. We started talking about our parents. Since my dad had just passed away, I told stories about him and teared up. This openness paved the way for our friends to get vulnerable too.

I knew Julie had absent parents. Her dad had mental health challenges and other issues and wasn't present for her today or for her children.

"I cried when our daughter didn't include her grandpa on the family tree they made at school."

Though the particulars of our story differed, I also knew what it was like to have a complicated relationship with parts of my family tree.

"Can we just cut off a branch?" Julie asked, half joking, half serious.

I thought for a minute and shared a bit about the research I was doing on intergenerational trauma and what can be done about it and said, "Yes."

"Yes, we can cut off a branch and start again. We can grow a new tree." This doesn't necessarily have to mean completely cutting off a family member and not having a relationship with them at all—but it can.

As I've been outlining in this book, the rhythms that can help us disrupt unhealthy patterns of trauma in our family trees can also help us grow new trees out of old stumps and set healthy boundaries with unhealthy family members. Just because the latest science may point to our DNA structure changing after trauma and being passed down to our descendants (epigenetics), this does not have to be the end of the story. Even though I've been connected—or better, tethered—to my own mother's story, this is not the end of things. Even though Heather experienced unspeakable tragedy, confusion, and grief, hers is a story that's still being written.

There are other chapters waiting on the tips of our pens. There is a sequel that can connect to those old roots and then pull them out to make space to plant something new (like the one I hope Heather is writing). And my own children, my own son and daughter? Your children or other family and friends whose lives you impact? They do not have to live a wink of it. The part of the tree that brings trauma doesn't have to extend to them if you see and work on your trauma. There are tools, like the practices of spiritual formation just outlined and the larger rhythms of this book, that propel us forward into freedom from trauma.

I love scrolling my social media feed to find a picture of Heather's family today. Her children. Grandchildren. There is such hope and love in their round, brown eyes. There is a light that dances like a waltzing prism hanging from a window.

When I think of Heather today, I am reminded not of the trouble or heartbreak of her story, but the love. Waiting, leading, hoping, dreaming, rejoicing with her. The new. The real. *Healing.* Believing that God loves and holds us all no matter what.

Five Actions You Can Take: Lean In to the Struggle

- Sit with another person you trust and share a part of your story that you've never told anyone before.
- Write a list of things you would do if you had no fear (travel, vocation, relationship, goal, hobby, etc.).
- Host a "Dig Deeper" meal with a friend or a small group of friends and commit to having intentional conversations about the real, the gritty, the struggles, and the joyful.
- Ask someone else about a time when they felt courageous. Listen to their story.
- Finish this journal prompt:

  Times when I have leaned in to and embraced the struggle are times when . . .

Rhythm 4

Get Real—Soul Honesty

Interlude 3

Daisies and Breaking Hearts

I first saw him on the crowded dance floor of the popular bar that I sometimes frequented with my roommates. The bar reeked of cigarette smoke, and the music blared, as guys stood around small high tables pretending to talk to each other. Groups of girls danced, their eyes darting to the guys to see if anyone noticed them.

He had sandy hair and warm, friendly eyes and was wearing a muted plaid green coat. I got a whiff of Old Spice as he passed me. I thought to myself that I'd like to meet someone that looked as nice as him. Shortly after that, he asked me to dance.

His male roommates thought I was the perfect girlfriend. I seemed to be always available to do the activities Gordon wanted and got along well with all his friends. And at each visit to their apartment, I attacked the pile of dirty dishes that had accumulated around the sink. The guys ate a lot of pizza, with all the dried-up crusts and bits of red sauce, onions, and mushrooms on the dirty plates. I bravely washed and dried the dirty mess, as the men appeared to look on approvingly. I thought that was what I was supposed to do.

Our relationship progressed, and I found myself realizing that his dream of living in the country and building a house wasn't the dream I saw for my future. I had grown up on the farm and was thoroughly enjoying all the activities and social life that the city had to offer. I loved the bright lights along the streets and above the shop doors at night and was totally amazed by the variety of people I saw and met. The small shops were full of things I'd never seen before, some even from different countries: fruity smelling soaps and long flowing colorful dresses. I loved to sit in the small coffee shops and listen to their new music I'd never heard with my shag haircut. (What if my parents knew I was a hippie?)

Gordon came over one night to pick me up for a date. As he came into my and my roommates' tiny downtown apartment, I pulled him around the small fake veneer partition that separated our kitchen from the bedroom. We stood silently huddled at the foot of my bed, trying to get some privacy. I stared at his plaid coat for a while, trying to get the courage to talk.

I finally cleared my throat and told him that I thought we were too different to stay together. I felt it was best to move on with our lives. I looked up at his face and saw his eyes glisten with silent tears. His breath had stopped and was now coming in short spurts. All he said was, "If you don't love me, then nobody will." It was at that second that I made a decision to stay with him. How could I possibly leave him alone without any love?

Why couldn't I say no? Where was my courage?

We didn't break up that night, and I never entertained the thought of leaving him again.

In fact, we started making plans to get married. I made those plans alone, making arrangements for the service in the small university chapel on campus and a catered reception of sandwiches, salads, and cake at a nearby park. I invited only our immediate families. My parents weren't at all excited, and my dad let that be known. He hated Gordon's long hair, bell-bottoms, and rusty light green van. That didn't matter to me, but I couldn't deny the putrid exhaust smell it gave out sometimes. My parents also gave the stipulation that they wouldn't attend the services unless we were married in the Catholic Church. Gordon agreed, and my parents were satisfied, though I really didn't care. My uncle, a priest, was going to officiate.

We were married on a beautiful day in June. I got up early that day and found my way to a tiny hair salon on a small side street near our apartment. I had found the salon a few days ago and thought it looked decent. It was nothing fancy, but the walls were a brightly colored green with a few yellow chairs strategically placed.

As I entered the salon, I saw her. She was an older woman who had a high, fake, dark beehive hairdo. I made a mental note that if I had seen her the day I had made the appointment, I would have run the other way. I told her it was my wedding day, but I could tell that she wasn't the least bit interested. She didn't make eye contact and muttered something I couldn't understand under her breath. I knew I was her first appointment of the day, as she was clutching her first cup of coffee and taking occasional sips. I was hoping she would just chug it all down, for maybe then she'd be in a better mood. I wanted someone to be happy with me. But deep down I knew that this was not the life I wanted. Why was it so hard for me to say no? Why couldn't I be honest?

As I slowly walked back to my apartment, I tried to visualize this as the blissful wedding day that it was supposed to be.

I was supposed to be surrounded by happy family who were admiring my dress, telling me how beautiful I looked and how my face glowed. Instead, I was putting on my dress by myself and dusting the dirt off my feet before I put on my boots. I was alone in my apartment, telling myself how happy I was, how perfect my life was going to be.

I wore a long, white gauzy dress with a ruffle at the bottom and short, white plastic boots. I didn't have enough money for the real leather ones that I wanted but didn't think anyone would notice them anyway. Gordon wore a lilac-colored shirt with a purple textured tie. I thought we looked the part for our wedding. Dressed up a bit but not too formal.

Pictures were taken on the chapel steps by one of Gordon's friends. I clung to Gordon's arm and smiled happily, as I watched groups of university students pass by. I imagined them thinking what a great couple we made and how perfect we looked together. Nobody told us that. I tried really hard to get to that blissful place that day, but I never got there. We spent the night on cold, musty-smelling, old sleeping bags in the back of his van. He had parked it on his land, next to the cement foundation for his house. All his dreams in one place.

Our marriage lasted one and a half years. I felt like a failure but didn't feel like I was breaking a sacred commitment. I can't say why. When my divorce lawyer's receptionist asked me why we were getting divorced, I said that we were too different to stay together. She asked why we couldn't stay and try to work things out. I said we had tried.

My parents had not come to visit us since our wedding day, but they came to our divorce hearing. I was completely supported in that decision. They even took me out to lunch, and as we ate, it became clear why they were there. They quietly brought up the idea of having my marriage annulled under the Catholic Church. Had I ever thought of that? I wasn't sure what that meant, so they explained it to me. I told them I'd think about it, but in the end, I agreed. That would make them feel better, since they knew Gordon wasn't the "right one" for me. I went through the process, writing a summary of our marriage and how I felt about it. I soon got a letter from the Catholic diocese saying that it had been approved. Our marriage was declared null and void. It had never existed as a Catholic marriage. It never existed, the little paper said. One hundred dollars to say it never existed. I never did pay that bill.

—Mother

Chapter 12

Our Stories Are Bigger

I have been and still am a seeker, but I have ceased to question stars and books; I have begun to listen to the teaching my blood whispers to me.

—Hermann Hesse

When I became a mother and my beautiful twins were born, I let out a shriek as I lay on the metal table, oblivious to the pain and the basketball team of nurses, doctors, onlookers, and my coach-husband. I was surrounded by a room of white coats, yet my eyes fixed themselves on the tiny humans they held up, one and then two, from behind a bloody curtain.

"Ahhh! Welcome to the world!" I cried, as my daughter shrieked back in the same way, mirroring me. The first of countless examples of following my lead.

Next came my son, with a little bit more trouble, but ahh-hhh, they were here! My long-awaited, longed-for loves. Fulfilled dreams that brought a song to my heart like living poetry:

The earth-meaning
Like the sky-meaning
Was fulfilled.[64]

But first, before we get here: rewind.

When I lived in Michigan in my early twenties, I walked on the beach with my trusty pup, Mo, and dreamed about my life. I'd see a young family with a toddling baby on stubby legs exploring the sand. I'd notice how the man gripped his wife's hand and didn't look in my direction when our paths crossed. The familiar pit in my gut ached as St. Jude, the patron saint of lost causes, peered down from the clouds and shook his head, his saintly hipster beard blowing in the lake breeze.

This—a *whole* family—was the life I wanted.

This was the life I dreamed of.

Not the life I thought I was going to have.

I was too broken.

Dirty.

Incomplete.

I'd seen this life passing by me on the beach and in movies and in the childhood home of my best friend, Crystal, who married her high school sweetheart, and it never felt possible. It was always just out of reach, like that magnificent web that dangles between our house and a tall poplar in late summer, the spider's skills at weaving from the clouds, mindboggling.

By my midtwenties, it was impossible. I jumped from relationship to relationship, always with someone that didn't measure up. Either they didn't treat me well (you've read a couple of these examples already) or I didn't. I was never or rarely with anyone that wouldn't hurt me or that I truly loved. They weren't any more than a body to fill the space, ease the boredom, someone who could (falsely) help me feel loved. Lovable. Worthy. Or someone to just get drunk or high with. Even though there wasn't much left to damage, men were my kryptonite. Or a more apt metaphor: my dope.

Reader, I know you have your own ache (or series of aches). Maybe you sit here today, flipping these pages or swiping left on your e-book or listening to the audiobook and are thinking of that thing that you long for so deeply that it makes your insides hurt. Maybe the hole has been there so long that you've stopped believing that it will ever be filled. Maybe the thing that happened to you has led you to stop dreaming altogether. You can't even imagine that you can be more than your trauma.

If this is the case, I want to encourage you. *You can get to a place where the dreams come back.* Whether that is in a hospital room after having your babies pulled from your gaping belly or getting that five-years-sober coin, or whatever your specific dream may be. But before we talk about how to get to the good stuff, I need to share a bit more about what got me here. Brace yourselves—it isn't pretty.

Brené Brown defines addiction this way: "Addiction can be described as chronically and compulsively numbing and taking the edge off of feelings."[65]

While addiction took on many forms in my life, like a shapeshifter straight out of the latest season of *Stranger Things*, it was primarily this: a means to escape and numb myself to feeling the effects and symptoms of trauma—especially as I was re-traumatized again and again in active addiction.

Carrying addiction and its secrets is more than a burden. The insane planning and preparation, the petty things we did for cash to pay for addiction, taking us down into a swirling world of paranoia and dizziness and usually very poor choices—some that we remember. Most that we don't. The heaviest load.

I've heard addiction described in so many ways as a medical condition, disease, moral failing, genetic predisposition, fissure of the will, and more. It has been portrayed in the media in the sparkliest yet most stigmatizing of ways. It has been glorified in movie theaters, late-night YouTube channel searches, on Super Bowl commercials (drinking looks so fun). Yet it has ravished families, marriages, neighborhoods, and churches. It has flowed through the branches of family trees. More than likely, addiction has impacted you in one way or another too. If it hasn't yet, and I don't want to freak you out, then it still might.

I told much of my addiction recovery story in *Downstairs Church*. I'll relate it here again, though with a bit more brevity. It is encouraging when we can look at our whole story (even the tough parts and traumas).

Ages 0–11: Introduction to adverse childhood experiences such as divorce, neglect, the list goes on.

11: First drink.

14: Become aware of my alcoholic tendencies, i.e., really, really, really like getting messed up. Sexually assaulted at a party.

15: Start smoking cannabis and really, really, really like getting even more messed up.

15 (A little bit later): Try cocaine for the first time and am consumed. Unhealthy teen relationships, bumping hip-hop on country back roads.

16: Enter full-blown addiction status. Adolescent inpatient addiction treatment.

17: Overdose. Adolescent inpatient addiction treatment
(again). Enter disordered eating and bulimia (not fun).
18–24: Continue to struggle with alcohol and cannabis
use off and on. Another sexual assault coming home
from a bar as a college student. Lots of sexual partners.
(By lots, I mean like *Sex and the City*'s Carrie numbers,
not Samantha, in case you are judging.)

Low self-worth.
Doubts about God.
Doubts about life.
Lack of purpose.
Confusion.
Shame.
Isolation.
Depression.
Anxiety.
Undiagnosed post-traumatic stress disorder.

I'll stop there, but you get the point. My earlier years were
rife with struggle: substances and the symptoms of trauma,
which for me manifested itself in almost zero boundaries and
the belief that perhaps all I was good for and indeed what all
men expected (and deserved) was my clothes off and in a heap
on a dirty carpet. My relationships with men were overrun
with those elements that make me shudder today (and would
send any innocent father of tweens and teens hurtling toward
an early grave).

When we talk and are honest about our history and how
trauma shows up in our lives, we are able to get real with ourselves, others, and God. Without soul honesty about all our

stories, we cannot move into transformative healing. Trauma isn't the end of our stories. I keep saying this because it is true. The ending doesn't have to be the pain we experienced. It can be a new beginning of hope even if we still carry the scars.

You may be wondering why I'm including this sordid timeline so far into this book, instead of at the beginning. I think it is important to remember that it's okay to carry the scars. As my friend Dr. Lee Warren says, "We get to live, but it leaves a mark." Just because we are on a healing journey does not mean we do not still carry scars. But today, we don't have to hold them. They don't have to define us. We can get honest and be free.

The Long Relapse

Addiction is "cunning, baffling, and powerful," as I've often heard it described in recovery circles. Or in faith circles, it's crouching, lying in wait, waiting to destroy someone (see 1 Peter 5:8). I know this firsthand because after three years of even religion-laden recovery, I relapsed on a sunny summer afternoon with a Blue Moon bottle and a Harley-riding farmer named John. Now, I'm not sure what was more tempting (the boy or the beer), but either way they both got the best of me.

As soon as I took the first drink, I started to crave alcohol like I had never stopped. That familiar feeling of millipedes on my skin and a twisting stomach resurfaced, reminiscent of how I'd ache for vodka on bus rides to high school if the other girls from my Midwestern small town didn't have any to share that morning.

During that time, I remember driving home from work, passing the gas station or Walgreens or even the Mexican restaurant with giant margaritas and almost stopping the car in the middle of the road to run out and pour as much alcohol as I could down my throat.

That period—the relapse or recurrence of use period, what I like to refer to as my Harley Davidson Days—lasted approximately five months. September 11, 2010 (hard to forget that date), until January 2, 2011 (my sobriety birthday). John and I enjoyed smoking Marlboro Lights while looking up at the night sky at his farm and taking in the smells of manure that made me feel at home (farm kids know what I'm talking about). We enjoyed drinking beer and taking long motorcycle rides up the eastern edge of Wisconsin, through touristy Door County to an island where it felt like we were the only ones alive on the planet. I remember on one of our trips, wishing we had brought more beer. I always wanted more. You might know the saying: *one is never enough.*

On Christmas Eve that year, we went out for dinner and I told myself I wasn't going to drink.

No way.

Not under any circumstances.

After dinner on our way back to his place, I asked where we could stop for beer and smokes.

"I thought you didn't want to drink tonight?" he asked with his innocent eyes.

I just nodded and whispered, "I changed my mind."

Holding the cold cans on my lap on the way home, I wondered how a six-pack was even going to come close to being enough. I decided that if I drank fast enough it might work and I might not get a hangover in the morning. It was going to be Christmas morning after all. I wondered how I could change my mind in an instant and go against what I so firmly wanted: to stay sober. As if I hadn't been through all this before.

We got back and he put on a movie, and I drank four of the beers in less than an hour and then threw up. I was pissed at myself for not being able to drive home, but I was thankful I had my period so I didn't have to draw any boundaries that four beers in quick succession regularly undrew.

Fast forward several days and it was New Year's Eve, and I got a little black dress and my long hair was back to blond. I felt pretty self-conscious in the red lips and heels I rarely wore. I looked in the mirror and stared at the familiar stranger who peered back at me with her cat eyes. I felt like I was playing the role of someone I didn't know. Pretending. Trying to fit myself into a box that I or God had long ago blown apart.

I got drunk. Drunker than John.

He passed out on our hotel bed, face first with his boots on, and I stayed up and watched bad TV and ate cold nachos. The next morning, we drove to another party and he brought a cooler of beer for the hour and a half highway drive there. At one point, I pulled the mirror down in front of me and lingered, before saying out loud, "I feel like I'm fourteen again . . . What am I running from?" (John didn't hear or didn't care.)

In *This Here Flesh*, Cole Arthur Riley writes:

> When you become accustomed to pain, it is not unusual to, consciously or subconsciously, habitually weaken your capacity to experience pain. But as we become less perceptive of pain, we lose touch with other

sensations as well—awe and delight included. As psychological wisdom explains, it is difficult to control the targets of our numbing.[66]

That was the last day I drank.

Fast forward a decade and some distance (and a lot of change), and there I was, getting my little babies swaddled in hospital blankets with little pink and blue caps over their sweet nugget heads. The nurse helped my husband (of a little less than a year) place them gently next to me, one on each side of my face.

Incredible.

Miraculous.

Surreal.

Like so many times in my life, only this time for the right, amazing reason, I floated above myself. I smiled at the moving picture I was in—my life—and how it had changed into something I never thought it could be. I told myself like I did on my wedding day.

"Remember this moment."

I looked around and saw the faces of the nurses and smiling doctors and felt the warmth that my husband's presence always brings, and I felt the skin of my precious babies' cheeks up against my tears of joy. The lines of Psalm 126 came to mind:

> When the LORD restored the fortunes of Zion,
> we were like those who dreamed.
> Our mouths were filled with laughter,
> our tongues with songs of joy.
> Then it was said among the nations,
> "The LORD has done great things for them."

The LORD has done great things for us,
and we are filled with joy.
Restore our fortunes, LORD,
like streams in the Negev.
Those who sow with tears
will reap with songs of joy.
Those who go out weeping,
carrying seed to sow,
will return with songs of joy,
carrying sheaves with them.

It was a tremendous grace: my twin babies bursting forth from the tears of my childhood and teen and young adult life. At almost forty years old, something had happened in my heart to release the fear of relationships and the inability to accept love. To let go of the unlovely parts of my past experiences and my family's and my family before them. It was as if, in that moment of releasing two new human beings and souls into the world, God spoke to me: "It is possible to heal." The timeline of my life started to bloom. I could feel songs of joy breaking the ground like crocus in spring.

> What are you ready to be honest about and let go of? What are you ready to dream and hope for?

Writing your own timeline and getting real about the tough stuff can help to open you up to next-level healing. When we embrace our entire story with acceptance, something incredible happens. We start to practice honesty with ourselves, and it clears the way for love.

Writing Your Timeline*

This exercise helps you embrace the entirety of your story. This can be done first individually, then shared in person or virtually in the safety of a small circle of trusted friends or at least one other person, mentor, or counselor. The important part of this exercise is making sure you have supports in place and at least one trusted person to share with. As one of my dear friends likes to say, "Recovery is a we thing."

- Start with a journal or sheet of paper and write a list in chronological order of all the big life moments— tough stuff, horrible stuff, and also the good and shining moments. You can get creative using fun markers or colored pencils, maybe stickers too if you are feeling fancy. Or, if you are like me and craftiness is not a spiritual gift, a good old-fashioned piece of white paper and a black ballpoint pen work too.

- Notice as you go along how perhaps you weren't alone during moments of pain. Maybe God placed a teacher or another safe adult in your path when you struggled as a child. Maybe as you look at the story of your life, you can see moments where love was there, where God showed up.

---

* I'd love to give a shout-out to my soul sister, Emily Killeen, who in 2020 started a virtual sober community called Recovery Revival. One of the exercises during a virtual meetup was to share our timelines. Doing this exercise, and then sharing it with a group of women, was incredibly healing. Thanks, Emily, for your insight and courage.

- I'd also like to encourage you to try the grounding exercises at the back of this book if you, like me, have experienced significant trauma and this exercise might be triggering.
- Again, this exercise is best in community and to be shared with another person. Getting real and learning soul honesty is also about letting others in and being known.

Every Other Weekends

My twins started getting older. When they were about two years old, which was the age I was when my mother left, I started to question again how and why my mom could bring herself to do a thing like leaving. I imagined her setting our little bodies down, watching as we tottered toward our grieving, shell-shocked dad, driving away, wondering every night how we were. Not being present. I couldn't dream of living a life where my babies weren't the absolute center around which I orbited like they were my sun.

Being able to analyze my childhood comes and goes. Just ask my therapist. I talked to my brother a bit, and he said he, too, went through something similar with his daughter, the question surfacing after years of childish confusion and Monster's silence. It's interesting as an adult; we learn that we don't have to accept things for what they are. We can say, "No, this isn't right." Even if there is nothing we can do to change the past. And what's more, sometimes we struggle with head-knowledge—the Bible verses and worship lyrics and well-intentioned advice—against the gravelly reality: heart truth.

When I was finally able to ask the question, "Why did you leave?"—or better, "*How* could you leave?"—I couldn't. She had already lived through so much. It was understandable. Even back then, before I started researching trauma and resilience and also what the Bible might have to say about it all, I knew that brokenness was generationally cyclical. I felt it in my blood. The pain comes round again and again. It is more than apparent when I look at my family tree, at my mother and father and her mother and father. There is some piece of our being human that is lost in the dash marks that connect us. Somewhere between life and death is where it can get muddled. Especially when those dashes are connected.

Sometimes my mom was a bright and shining figure, like a centaur with golden wings that swooped down and carried us above the clouds to McDonald's to get our Happy Meals and to Foot Locker to get the expensive sneakers that our dad would never go for, because who in God's name in 1992 would ever buy shoes for more than fifty bucks. When we weren't with her every other weekend, we dreamed of our hours-long car trips to wherever the new place was that had "a room for us so it felt like ours." We wanted to see her and share with her our weeks' worth of hurt or joy or kid-details that just had to be discussed with her, our parent-friend. The topics morphed over time from what my brother's favorite dinosaur was, to how I struggled with being bullied in school, to contraceptives.

My brother and I would spend the weekend, two half days driving, two nights, and one full day, visiting our mom like she was some distant relative or a friend of a friend's mom. But it was our life, and it was our reality, and it wasn't until we were older that we realized how crushing and confusing this was. How it impacted us.

The older we got, the harder it became. My brother and I clung to the little piece of stability that we gave each other, but this waned over time too. I remember feeling very much alone when puberty hit, not realizing there were other kids going through the same changes. "Divorce is in the machine now, like love and birth and death," says novelist Ann Patchett.[67] No wonder so many young people don't want to get married anymore when over 50 percent of marriages end in divorce.

My mother was beautiful back then and still is today. Blue eyes like my daughter. Blondish hair like me back then. A mix between Meg Ryan in *When Harry Met Sally* and Princess Diana. But when she cried, her face morphed and its beauty contorted. It was hard to witness. Maybe because I was a kid and I didn't know what to do about it. Like I was somehow responsible. Some weekends, she cried and cried. Some weekends, she said she tried a new medicine and it was better. Some weekends, she tried to explain (again) why she was leaving her husband (again) and finding a cute little apartment (again) that would have room for us (again) if we wanted to visit or even move in with her.

Over time, my brother and I stopped letting my mother's various men into our lives in a genuine way. It was too painful. We didn't understand it all. How could we? But we did start to learn more about words like trauma and power and intimacy. We started to understand that there was something broken about our childhood. We watched other kids with their two parents and no place to travel to for "visitation" every other weekend, the after-effects being like some medieval torture device, nibbled inch by inch by hungry mice. Another hole in our gut.

My brother found mom-figures: teachers, parents of friends; and I just sulked, never feeling much like connecting with anyone anyway. What's the point? "It's sad, something coming to an end. It cracks you open, in a way—cracks you open to feeling. When you try to avoid the pain, it creates greater pain." This is what Jennifer Aniston said to *Vanity Fair* in 2006 after her separation from Brad Pitt.[68]

There is a verse of scripture in the book of Matthew that answers this question: how can we move from heavy to light, from the weight of the world (divorce, trauma, addiction, etc.) to freedom?

> Come to me, all you who are weary and burdened, and I will give you rest. Take my yoke upon you and learn from me, for I am gentle and humble in heart, and you will find rest for your souls. For my yoke is easy and my burden is light. (Matthew 11:28–30)

Jesus will help us with the weight of what we carry like an Uber driver with Southern manners? Even though in exchange for this rest, there is another yoke (i.e., we still need bags if we are going somewhere), Jesus promises that because of his gentle and humble spirit, a new rest can be found? If I'm honest, a part of me resists the simplicity.

What about my past? What about my hurt? What about my mother? I've learned that I've had to ask these painful questions over and over again, questions where a simple Bible verse isn't enough. I've had to dig in with a therapist, in community, and in recovery, analyzing these questions and being honest with myself.

Understanding our stories is about more than just being honest about our mistakes or unhealthy patterns; it's about looking long and carefully, taking it all in, at what we are feeling and why, when we've made those mistakes. Such an effort has an outcome of metabolizing the pain in a way that addiction never can. It can move us to a place where we can experience living in recovery.

When I look at the honest timeline of my life and how God has shown up, how recovery has transformed my life, and how I have been able to, one rhythm at a time, disrupt the cycle of trauma from my past and my family, for me, there is no question: transformation is possible.

It's not just me. I've worked with so many women, and met others while speaking at churches and conferences, who share their own incredible testimonies of transformation that happen after they got honest about their stories and accepted all of it with open hands.

It's not easy when we share our timelines, examine the painful roots of our past, or admit how much we may have in common with our parents. Yet, with each step forward of getting real, we are one step closer to healing, one step further along the journey of becoming ourselves.

Chapter 13

Puddles of Mascara

God comes to us disguised as our life, wooing us through our misery toward surrender.

—Heather Kopp, *Sober Mercies*

Today, I sat outside on the front porch swing with my mother and had one of those moments that are coming more frequently now as she is getting older. It's like a reverse déjà vu. In an instant, as I'm looking into her paling blue eyes that still have that same glisten, I realize that when she is gone, this is how I will remember her and our time together. So easy. Natural.

After I hit twenty and realized that my mom was actually a person of her very own with hopes, desires, dreams, longings, we became really good friends. Most Friday evenings and sunny Saturday mornings or Sunday afternoons, we'd "hit the town" as we'd say and laugh with our eyes and go to Barnes & Noble (https://www.barnesandnoble.com/blog/) and buy blank notebooks we intended on journaling in and drank chai tea lattes long before matcha tea was a thing. Or we would go to the student union on the University of Wisconsin–Madison campus, the one by Lake Mendota dotted with green, yellow, and orange chairs, and wear our matching long flower skirts (during our hippie phase) and giggle about boys and PMS and good sex and good ice cream and all those things that mothers and daughters don't discuss in some households, but we did.

It was amazing and I felt loved and understood. We recognized how similar we were even then. It was fresh air—our friendship—especially after the rotten hell of my adolescence before I forgave her for leaving us as kids. Those screaming matches and rage-tears—by the time we were strolling in our skirts, sipping our tea, and ogling the same-aged men, those memories from my teen years were long gone. She didn't have to try to discipline me anymore with her soft style. My heart softened to her experience because I was living it too.

It was around this time that I learned how hard it was for her growing up. She started to fill in the gaps of what I recalled hearing murmurings about. Why she started volunteering in the '90s for an organization in Madison that put on Take Back the Night rallies advocating for survivors of domestic and sexual abuse. Why she chose to sit in circles with other women who shared their stories of trauma with groups of perpetrators who looked on with icy looks or quiet tears or wailing.

I remember a story she told me one sunny afternoon as we sat near the lake and sipped our tea. As she spoke, it was as if she became the little girl, as if the memory was happening in the present or I was reading her secret journal:

"If your thighs rub together when you walk, you weigh too much." These words echoed in my mind.

I can still hear it: "You're so thin. Have you lost weight?"

I try to hide my satisfaction that someone notices. I am proud to be thin. It feels good to be getting attention from my family, from our father. See how much control I have. It feels good to have so much control over something.

It is Thanksgiving Day and our family is gathering at the farm. I've been dieting for a while now, and I can tell I've lost weight. My black pants hang loosely around my hips. My face looks tight and drawn. What only matters is that I look thin.

I want to be the thinnest.

That's always the goal.

I glance around the table at the small mounds of food on old porcelain.

My fork shifts potatoes from one corner of the plate to the other.

I eat slowly. Take small bites. I never feel full anymore. I always have the same empty feeling.

I'm used to it.

I'm hungry.

I learned that my mom and I had been through much of the same things, though these same things had different levels of intensity and duration (like really awful HIIT workouts on YouTube). Though some of the details were different, we could relate to the feelings and to the aftermath: the debris that the storms of trauma left in their wake.

Numbness.

Isolation.

Fear.

Loneliness.

Shame.

Self-loathing.

Self-harm.

Starvation.

Replays.

We didn't have to go into many specifics. We just understood. We'd sip our lattes and cry or laugh and hold on to each other before parting: the best hug ever. Nothing beats a hug from your mom.

At one of the Take Back the Night events, my mom had the courage to read a poem she wrote about someone who had hurt her. Even though not everyone in her life believed her (believed them) at the time, she shared her story, one little lightning bolt at a time. It struck stone places in the audience, giving permission for mutual, trembling remembrance and courage. Her words lit fear up like a pile of dry August straw. It burned and burned.

The poem was called "Dancing on His Grave."

Years later, after one of the people who had hurt her had died, she called me one night.

"I went for a drive today to the cemetery. And I finally did it. I danced."

Hungry

It's tough to get honest. One of the first mentors I had in recovery was also in recovery from disordered eating. She was one of the first people to introduce me to the idea that my "food issues" were connected to my trauma. She also helped me to recognize the patterns that I was repeating of my mother's. If recovery is a "we thing," then trauma can be too. It wasn't only my mentor either. The more I started talking about my unhealthy relation-ship with food with other women in recovery and the more I listened, the more it became clear that this was something ram-pant among survivors. We are hungry. We are full. Food can become a weapon, another way to hurt ourselves.

I remember staring at myself in the mirror after purging (sticking my finger or a toothbrush or anything down my throat to induce a gag reflex). My face flushed, my heart fluttered, and a single tear fell, taking a puddle of mascara with it.

My mother eating only rice and chocolate shakes.

Staring in the mirror as a size three and seeing fat, loath-some fat.

How the body hangs on to spiritual sickness.

How the hurting are hungry for love.

According to the American Psychological Association, trauma is:

> An emotional response to a terrible event like an acci-dent, rape, or natural disaster. Immediately after the event, shock and denial are typical. Longer term reac-tions include unpredictable emotions, flashbacks, strained relationships and even physical symptoms like headaches or nausea. While these feelings are normal, some people have difficulty moving on with their lives.[69]

"Having difficulty moving on with their lives" is an under-statement for those of us who know. That's like saying some-one who survives military combat or a volcano eruption or a 9.5 earthquake will have trouble "adjusting."

For those who know—you may be one of us—trauma and traumatic experiences can become a part of who we are, especially if we don't have the protective factors to help guard against the damage and aftershock. That's why it hasn't, for me, been something I can just pack up the van and drive away from. As I've said before in other ways, it's been a slow decluttering and throwing away. It's taken me years to figure out that it all goes a lot faster when there are many hands involved.

But we can get stuck here too. We can get stuck on the notion that there is no escaping the symptoms, the trauma, or its effects. There is the faulty notion that "I'll always be like this" or "I'll never find a good man" or "I'll never deserve to be happy" or fill in the blank with your favorite.

This used to be one of my favorites: "I'll always be crazy."

Cue Patsy Cline.

God, I love that song.

Such a desperate place to be in. I remember, and I can almost feel you cringe at my use of the word "crazy." I can sympathize with those who feel like there is no way out of that label because I've been there. All the issues: addiction, disordered eating, unhealthy relationships, boundaries issues—all of it, the weight of it, bearing down. Even if you have not experienced these particular things, you know how much the past can creep into the present. How much that event (whether it be a natural disaster, job loss, family loss, combat experience, or other heartbreak) nestles itself in and builds a home. It might take years for it to construct a permanent dwelling in your mind, but it happens. And it feels like it will never leave.

"Life is a school in which we are trained to depart," Henri Nouwen said.[70] And how very true this is. There are always goodbyes and endings. This is life, after all. And none of us are exempt from the final goodbye. But for some reason, all the yuck, all the mess, at different points in my life felt too much a part of me to escape. It took me a long time to realize that for my family of origin, for my mother, it's been the same. The same things I've had a difficult time letting go of, like addiction and the other emotional, physical, and spiritual consequences of trauma, like disordered eating, have gripped my mother's life too. And who knows how many generations before her.

Trauma has a tendency to do this: solidify things. Like a piece of pottery in a kiln that's been shaped and formed and now the heat and fire is cementing the glaze so that the colors and textures last. It's a long process or a slow undoing to change the piece of art that comes from the kiln. Sometimes, in fact, the only way to change it is to smash it to bits.

> What are some of the ways that trauma has manifested itself in your life or is present today? Do you recognize the patterns passed down from generations before you? Do you have things, like my mother and me, that you share in common with your own mother or father or grandparent? Have you heard stories about the great-uncles who had alcoholism or gambled a lot or the great-grandma who was single and died young, unexplained? What are you hungry for?

It can be sad when we take a closer look into the branches of our family trees and get honest about ourselves and our family histories. Yet we can be sad *and* grateful. That's the thing about pain and suffering; it can bring you not only to a place of healing but to a banquet of tremendous thankfulness.

Chapter 14

Doing Hard Things

You are not out of time and there is still room for you to explore what it means to unfold into your bloom.

—Morgan Harper Nichols

Let's continue this journey of letting go and getting real. Let's continue to disrupt the patterns of trauma in our lives.

But before we continue, I want to say how proud I am of you. You are working your way through this book! You are committing to healing. You have an honest desire to free the generations that come after you so that they do not have to repeat your family trauma patterns. This is remarkable. You may not be used to giving yourself kudos, so let me do this for you. I am so very proud of you.

I also want to take a moment for a little confession of my own. Like I shared way back in the introduction of this book, my journey is not finished. What I preach, I practice on the good days and struggle to do on the rough ones. Though I write about solutions and have shared these rhythms, I'm not always living in them.

I'm walking this journey with you, guiding you and at the same time moving step-by-step. We are in this together.

While we are continuing to get real and honest, I want to admit next that I've struggled personally with the content I'm about to dive into. These concepts may be startling, offensive, and ridiculous. These two words might feel for you, in the context of what we are talking about here, like Trauma (with a capital T)—wrong, in poor taste. Like dropping the F-bomb on Sundays.

We'll start with the slightly more palatable concept first: Confession. Let's take a peek inside the book of James: "Therefore, confess your sins to each other and pray for each other so that you may be healed. The prayer of a righteous person is powerful and effective" (James 5:16).

If you've followed along for a while as part of my email community, I've quoted this verse many times because it is such a foundational one for me. As a Christian convert who came to the faith later in life (after I could legally purchase a cheap bottle of wine from a gas station), the book of James stands out to me as a book that is both practical and easy to read. I imagine James as a burly and reasonable type with dark eyes and big hands like a renovator on HGTV. This man is about action.

James (outside of my imagination) is thought to be the half brother of Jesus who did not become a follower until after the resurrection. He was one of the major heads of the church in Jerusalem and called a "pillar of the church" by his bro, Paul (Galatians 2:9). He fought mightily for the inclusion of gentiles as Christ followers and took part in a big fancy meeting of the minds (think the modern-day G7 Summit) to determine a bunch of stuff like whether non-Jewish Christians had to observe Jewish law and painful Jewish customs like circumcision. His letter, as we know it today, was penned sometime before this meeting was to happen in the city of Jerusalem.*

This time in history also illuminates the concept of radical grace. I love how spiritual writer Max Lucado puts it: "Grace is the voice that calls us to change and then gives us the power to pull it off."[71] Grace moves toward inclusion, embraces, and swallows up everything it sees in love. Even the weak. Even the broken. Especially the traumatized. Despite the contradiction of what you may see on protest posters, this was one of the main pillars of the early church then and the modern-day church now: Grace. This grace, Philip Yancey writes, is "like water" and "flows to the lowest part."[72]

Chuck Swindoll from Insight for Living Ministries states that "the book of James looks a bit like the Old Testament book of Proverbs dressed up in New Testament clothes."[73] It focuses on the practicality of the gospel, how faith can and should be walked out in the context of grace. Healing and faith are not just about believing; they are about spirit-driven action. And I'd like to argue that confession (especially for a recovering woman like me) is one of the primary ways of acting out one's faith and healing.

---

* As an aside (one that I find comical): It is not surprising that these dudes eventually decided that adult males did not need to be circumcised. It was all quite shocking, and perhaps a little unfair, for the Jewish men who had gone through with it. This whole situation may have had a different outcome if the women were in charge of making that decision. Just saying.

Getting Real

Interestingly, there is a long history of confession throughout the ages, including within other religions like Hinduism. It has been touted in the Catholic Church and is known as the Sacrament of Penance. Confession is also a part of our legal and judicial system and can be something that our kids do when we give them the stink eye or what we do when our kids give us the stink eye. Guilty as charged.

Let's back up a bit from James 5:16, as it begins with the word "therefore." This word is like a bridge of letters joining two important ideas. Anytime we see the word "therefore" in the Bible or anywhere for that matter, it's a signal to read the lines before "therefore" and then after.

Right before James talks about this confession bit, the New International Version labels this section "The Prayer of Faith." It reads:

> Is anyone among you in trouble? Let them pray. Is anyone happy? Let them sing songs of praise. Is anyone among you sick? Let them call the elders of the church to pray over them and anoint them with oil in the name of the Lord. And the prayer offered in faith will make the sick person well; the Lord will raise them up. If they have sinned, they will be forgiven. Therefore confess your sins to each other and pray for each other so that you may be healed. The prayer of a righteous person is powerful and effective. (James 5:13–16)

Here, James talks about faith (the verb) and what it looks like.

What do the faithful do?

Pray.

Praise.

Anoint.

Confess.

Intercede.

There is much to unpack here. These verses are like the ginormous light brown suitcase that my family brings with us on our trips. As a single, working woman, I used to stuff it full of cute dresses and boot options, but now have to share with two other humans. In other words, there's a lot here. I don't have time or space to address all these ideas, but I would like to point out the emphasis on confession.

It is after all these things—prayer, praise, anointing, healing—that confession shows up after the summary word "therefore." James says, because of all these things—the praying and singing and praising and healing—we must confess so that we can get our hearts ready to receive.

Receive what?

Healing.

Community welcomes us to open ourselves to vulnerability. To open ourselves to hurt. To open ourselves to sharing in the sufferings of others and to see that we are not alone in our experiences. To open ourselves up to confession, to getting real. When we are able to let go of the cloak of shame that wraps us tightly in the labels of "damaged" and "broken" and "bad," we can start to move a little more freely. Think changing from boa-constricting yoga pants to comfy joggers (praise the Lord). Hugging the ankle, letting thighs breathe.

After learning how to share—or confess—we begin to move a little more freely in our experiences and not be bound by them any longer. When something is out in the open, what was once hidden turns into something else. It is no longer an experience to cause shame, but an experience that creates connection.

Let's give it a try now.

I'll go first.

When I was fourteen years old, I stole liquor from the woman I babysat for (my stepmom's good friend), invited a whole hoard of soon-to-be high schoolers over, and mixed everything I could find in the cupboards with diet Mountain Dew in a gas station slurpy cup. Two hours later, I was puking out the side of a senior boy's Camaro, fluorescent orange chunks flying through the air, hitting the door, my hair, and rolling fields of corn right before harvest.

When I was in college, I was so poor (buying cannabis was way more important than buying personal care items) that I'd bring an extra big backpack to campus and stuff it with rolls of toilet paper that I'd steal from gray-tiled bathrooms between classes. Trust me, it is no fun wiping your butt with a coffee filter.

As a young woman, I spent thousands of hours with men (boys) that I didn't like because I was lonely and afraid of silence and aching for love.

And that's just a start. Thankfully, I've been able to get so much out, sharing with sponsors and mentors and friends and family and complete strangers on my blog. It's cathartic like spring rain. Freeing like love. Comforting like a cat's purr.

Manda Carpenter in *Soul Care to Save Your Life* says, "Radical honesty leads to radical healing. Radical honesty is exactly that: radical. It's not just telling the truth when it's easy; it's about searching for the truth and going out of our way to dig up anything that is untrue."[74]

Okay, your turn.

And let me remind you: this isn't an exercise in futility. It is an exercise in freedom.

> Try this journal prompt: *Today, I'm ready to get real about . . .*
> You can take this exercise to the next level by sharing it with someone you trust and then inviting them to do the same.

Willing Surrender

When Cheryl Strayed was out on the Pacific Crest Trail, with Monster (if you recall, the very large pack that she hauled on her petite frame) for ninety-four days, some days felt painfully redundant. Her purpling toenails, brittle and chipping off the flesh, the blisters, the hard ground, the rain that soaked to the bone. But this epic adventure, in all of its uncomfortability, became more than a series of experiences, it became her memoir.

In an interview for *Author Magazine*, Cheryl talks about the process of writing her story.[75] She recounts what it was like to take the sometimes mundane actions of one foot in front of the other and create something of beauty and meaning for the reader. The memoir puts flesh on our experiences. When we explore our stories for its pain points, we are "out with lanterns, looking."[76]

My reading of her book was an experience. At times, I felt the hard rain, the fear of the unknown, the treacherous climbs, the aching legs. She carried me along with her storytelling so that I was experiencing the scene as if at the movies, watching and feeling. Yet, I also felt it deep in my soul. I related so much to her story and to her many moments of surrender along the rugged Pacific Crest Trail.

Cheryl surrendered much of her own struggles out on the PCT: her mother's death from cancer at forty-five, her addiction to heroin and men, her failed marriage. With each step, she let go of the monsters of her past. And through the writing of memoir, she invited us along toward our own moments of surrender and acceptance. Her words gave us permission to let go of our pain and our old story—and more than that, she begged us to welcome our joy.

"Don't surrender all your joy for an idea you used to have about yourself that isn't true anymore," she shares. And this led me to ask: can we play an active role in our own surrender or acceptance of our experiences, and will this surrender lead us toward greater healing? Can there be things about ourselves that aren't true anymore?

———

Dr. Stephanie Covington wrote a foundational and controversial book in the early 1990s called *A Woman's Way through the Twelve Steps*. She was one of the first researchers to understand that women needed something different in terms of recovery support for addiction and other challenges. Because of her work as a clinician, she understood that the trauma women experience can create unique challenges that are often roadblocks to healing. She also recognized that sometimes even the framing of particular ideas in particular ways (like the concept of surrender, itself) can be triggering and disempowering for people who have experienced trauma.

When a friend introduced me to her work, it was a pivotal point in my journey. The concepts of powerlessness and surrender and submission were not welcome ones. My mom understood this too. When we've experienced things that have taken away our power and control and agency over our own lives and bodies, the thought of going to that place again to get healthy is a triggering one.

Submit?

Surrender?

Admit I'm powerless?

No, thank you.

You may hear these words too and remember what it's like to give in to something.

No choice.

No control.

No power.

Boundaries toppling over.

Doors being pushed in.

We may not have positive associations with some of these terms that feel archaic and irrelevant and downright damaging.

The idea of submitting to a higher power or God can be equally challenging too. Especially if you are like me and your healing journey is intimately connected to your faith journey. Throughout scripture and in traditional twelve-step literature like *The Big Book* of Alcoholics Anonymous or the workbooks of Celebrate Recovery, we are shown pathways of healing through language that can be tough for some of us.

Here is another example from the book of James:

Submit yourselves, then, to God. Resist the devil, and
he will flee from you. Come near to God and he will
come near to you. Wash your hands, you sinners, and
purify your hearts, you double-minded. Grieve, mourn
and wail. Change your laughter to mourning and your
joy to gloom. Humble yourselves before the Lord, and
he will lift you up. (James 4:7–10)

Did that first word—"submit"—get caught in your throat
too?

While this word is tough for me, the contemporary editor
in me loves how this idea is framed and followed next by a
series of simple action verbs: resist, come near, wash, purify,
grieve, mourn, wail, and humble ourselves. James knew what
it meant to write for the reader. I also love how this verse ends
with humility followed by a "lifting up." Humility being, as I've
heard shared by old-timers in recovery meeting rooms, "not
thinking less of yourself, but thinking of yourself less." So if we
follow along, as James suggests, may we come to a place of
empowerment and be lifted up?

"God is with me."

"Be still and know that I am God."

"I know God is in control."

The most trusting statements of utter faith and surrender
that I've ever heard are from women who have experienced
immense pain yet accepted that something outside of themselves could support their healing.

I'd met Alma when she lived in a recovery home for
women, where members of our church visited, brought

personal care items, and planned social events and activities. Her long black hair, piercing black eyes, thick black eyeliner, and red lips portrayed a soft look when you'd expect the opposite. Alma had seen some things. She'd been a part of some things. And when I say "some things," I mean the excruciating kind of trauma that follows childhood sexual abuse, drug addiction, and years of sex work and damaging relationships with men and women. Alma's life was a mosaic of shattered hope. Despite this, like other women I'd met along this journey, Alma's faith was iridescent.

Alma had been around the church and recovery for a while and then strayed again, being allured by the familiar life of pain and crisis. After a couple years of back and forth, she found herself again sober, carrying her Bible and wanting more for her life and her future with her son. I noticed how she had been posting on social media about an upcoming challenge, about how she knew she needed to trust God and how she felt entirely surrendered to God's will for her.

Her faith inspired me, similar to the way Cheryl Strayed's hike and memoir inspired me.

Though at that time I had over a decade living in recovery, it wasn't the faith of the "old timer" that inspired me most; it was the faith of the newcomer. The one closest to the struggle who was able to yet say, "I believe." And "I am more."

I reached out and asked how she was doing, and a couple of texts later I found out that she was waiting for her trial. Some things had happened during her last recurrence of use, and they had finally caught up with her. She refused to lay the blame on anyone else, so she was likely facing jail, if not prison time, for a string of charges.

We met for a meeting and as I hugged her, the smell of ocean mist body spray and cigarettes took me back to when I'd faced something similar, familiar. For me, it wasn't incarceration, but it was like waiting over an abyss, a trust fall that led to freedom. For Alma, she knew she had to surrender to the consequences she was facing because in facing them, there existed the possibility of a new life, an honest life.

Alma reminded me of the beauty of surrender and the statement "Not my will, but yours be done."

The concept of submission, then, can be more. It can be bigger than just the idea of being out of control and needing to reach out for something more or someone to help. Along the road to recovery, we can surrender to the consequences of our actions or the fallout from others' actions. We can commit to accepting all the pieces of our stories and take responsibility where it is ours to accept. Dr. Covington recognized this and has been involved in creating evidence-based resources for women and other folks, including those who are incarcerated. She's been able to articulate the truth that within some of these ideas, including submission to a power greater than us, there is a freeing place that doesn't have to trigger trauma. Alma and so many women like her have shown me this and are living examples of true faith through acceptance.

Surrender is saying yes to this truth and no to the darkness. Taking our trauma lens off, we can see this clearly. Surrender opens up a new way to *turn toward*, that is cleared by healing and love. What's even more beautiful and what many of us learn through the recovery process is that shared surrender and being radically honest to the very core of our souls can free these sacred places too. There is so much power in the shared human story and soul honesty.

Five Actions You Can Take: Get Real

- Share with a friend or write about a time you longed for something that didn't happen on your desired schedule. What was it like in the waiting?
- What are some words that come to mind when you think about your *whole* story?
- Watch a documentary like *The Anonymous People*[77] or read stories from people in recovery on my story-telling platform, Circle of Chairs[78] (hearing personal stories of recovery can help reduce the stigma all of us may carry to varying degrees—even those of us in recovery).
- Write your own timeline (see earlier instructions) and encourage a friend to write theirs too and exchange stories over coffee or tea.
- Finish this journal prompt:

  For me, being real looks like . . .

Rhythm 5

Let God—Living Open-Handed

Chapter 15

Golden Refuse

The trauma said, "Don't write these poems.
Nobody wants to hear you cry about the grief inside your bones."
—Andrea Gibson

The spring my twins were two years old, we decided to take a trip north to Wisconsin to visit my parents and a few friends. It would have been stressful even without two toddlers. Days of driving on loud highways; expensive fast food with two main ingredients: salt and sugar; packing, unpacking, then packing again; in and out of Airbnb's that smelled like hotel mixed with the faint whiff of a wet cocker spaniel.

We made it to the final destination of our trip (thank God), and the memory is so strong, and so *good*, that I'd like to take you there with me for just a moment . . .

We end up finally staying at my mother's childhood farm. It was bought and renovated by one of her sisters and sits vacant most days of the year. Inside, it is pristine and decorated by a woman with impeccable taste and the funds to back that up. All variations of the same brown and expensive wood and wrought iron and paintings of cows and pigs and roosters and blond girls hanging clothes on the line. And did I mention roosters? Wooden ones and metal ones and stone ones and colored ones and ones made of straw or grass.

I sit on a tall chair covered in the softest leather and glance out the window at the most beautiful sun setting into emerald hills. The way they curve, it reminds me of a woman lying on her side—that point where hips roll into thighs. The sun—oh the sun—how it shines. If I squint my eyes and look toward it, I can see light that pierces out of the center like rays piercing the earth. Like St. Catherine of Siena holding out her saint hands, a rainbow of blessing. I blink and little balls of light flutter behind my eyelids. This is why you're not supposed to look at the sun.

But it is so beautiful.

I take a deep breath and hear the air hit my teeth as I exhale. Our twins are sleeping upstairs. I can finally take a minute to just be a person and not someone who is always doing something. Not a mom. Not a wife. Not a woman in recovery. Just a me. I can sink into another memory—or, better, the feeling of a memory—and not get stuck. I can trace my finger along the immensity of a thousand farm fields stretching across the landscape like an elongated psalm.

On vibrant evenings like this, if I were a bird, I would be one of the singing ones. Not a sunrise singer, but a sunset one, right before the world is covered in a blanket of dark and stars and calm. One last look at the miracle and brilliance of day with a melody. My birdsong, an aching tune, like a song by Nina Simone. Something you have to move your body to like waves in the sea.

I step outside to take a picture of the sunset with my phone because (of course) I have to take a picture with my phone, and the cold air hits my face and socked feet. I take another deep breath through my nose and this time the farm smell hits, the sweet smell of home for me. Every time I've come home to Wisconsin and that smell hits me (yes, "that smell" means manure), the stinky-sweet brings back memories—the good ones—without really bringing them back.

Do you have those places from your childhood that bring back memories? Like when you see the cover of *Goodnight Moon*, the illustrations and lines flood back into your brain as you stare at the strange, smooth, orange and green pages. Do you have those moments that themselves hark back to another time that almost every part of you has forgotten, yet somewhere in the basement of your mind, they rest, dusty?

When growing up, we stopped going to the farmhouse for about a decade, somewhere between elementary school and college. It began when my mother's parents showed up at her apartment door after her divorce from my dad. She told my brother and I to hide in the bedroom, and we heard voices rise louder and louder. Looking out of the bedroom, I saw my grandfather and his black shiny shoes through the crack in the door. I saw my grandmother's expression, always smeared on her face in the same color of matte foundation: *Barely There*. Her shimmering pink lips turned down like any good Catholic in distress.

"You have to leave. Don't come in." My mom cried frantically (as is her style of crying, especially when she's scared). We'd seen it before. Just not in this context. We'd see it again.

"Where are the children, Diana? What are you doing?" They were worried.

Then I heard muffled voices.

Door slam.

Why was she so afraid? Were we safe?

My mom ran toward where we were, and we looked at her the way we did back then all doe-eyed, with questions that we knew couldn't be answered. Not then. Not by her.

Dani Shapiro in *Hourglass: Time, Memory, Marriage* says:

> Years vanish. Months collapse. Time is like a tall building made of playing cards. It seems orderly until a strong gust of wind comes along and blows the whole thing skyward. Imagine it: an entire deck of cards soaring like a flock of birds.[79]

More Monsters

In the late 1990s, researchers looked at past literature on Holocaust survivors and their descendants while also studying the descendants of indigenous people living on reservations in the US. They created the term "historical trauma"[80] to describe what they saw happening among these two people groups who had experienced widespread trauma.

As a child, all I knew of indigenous peoples is what, sadly, I learned from the Disney movie *Pocahontas* and my favorite childhood book, *Island of the Blue Dolphins*. I recall hiking as a child with my mom when it was *her weekend* through parks along the Lake Mendota shoreline in Madison, Wisconsin, historically Ho-Chunk Nation land. I'd ask her about the mounds of dirt formed into shapes of animals like turtles and bears and horses. I learned that these mounds were ancient burial sites. The Ho-Chunk buried their dead in collective graves and created these incredible, tragic pieces of art on the earth. I don't ever remember asking my mom why there were so many dead. Why they had to have the mass graves in the first place.

What I'd learn later in life is more pieces, albeit incomplete, of what indigenous peoples have experienced. Most of it was shocking, too much for my white, privileged ears to hear. Tens of millions decimated either by murder, disease, or a combination of both, generations before. What some scholars say was the most horrific genocide in history.[81] The remaining families were forced to live in set places that were oftentimes poor farming land. Horrifically, the children, beginning in the mid-1800s, were sent to assimilation schools where they were taught to unlearn their culture and become part of the dominant group.

What is more, even as an adult living almost a half-century in the US, I am uninformed about the state of poverty, substance use disorders, and mental health conditions like post-traumatic stress disorder that so many indigenous peoples and reservations are plagued with today. I wouldn't know, according to the Substance Abuse and Mental Health Services Administration (SAMHSA), that these are some of the effects of historical trauma that linger for indigenous families and communities:

- A breakdown of traditional Native family values
- Alcohol and other substance abuse
- Depression, anxiety, and suicidality
- Child abuse and neglect and domestic violence
- Post-traumatic stress disorder
- General loss of meaning and sense of hope
- Internalized oppression, self-hatred[82]

Kathleen Brown-Rice, professor at the University of South Dakota states that:

> The theory of historical trauma was developed to explain the current problems facing many Native Americans. This theory purports that some Native Americans are experiencing historical loss symptoms (e.g., depression, substance dependence, diabetes, dysfunctional parenting, unemployment) as a result of the cross-generational transmission of trauma from historical losses (e.g., loss of population, land, and culture).[83]

But how does this happen? How can "historical loss symptoms be transferred to subsequent and current generations of indigenous communities?"[84] Of course, as in much of the world today, there are differing viewpoints. Some say it's all science. That epigenetics is at play too. The body and its functioning changes at the cellular level of DNA and then is passed down to family members—and this accounts for the impact of trauma done generations before. Others point to environmental causes, years of living with the results of trauma impacting one generation's ability to show up for another. Thus continuing the cycle, a nuanced version of the nature versus nurture argument. Still others point to a spiritual answer, that brokenness and trauma have a mystical element that haunts family trees. A theory that states maybe there is more at play here than what our eyes can see. I've come to wonder if maybe all have a contributing role: science and environment or nature and nurture, along with something happening in the spiritual realm that we do not have the words (or research studies) for, yet we know is true because our blood whispers it is so.

Those Genes Though

What is epigenetics?

The Centers for Disease Control and Prevention offers this definition:

> Epigenetics is the study of how your behaviors and environment can cause changes that affect the way your genes work. Unlike genetic changes, epigenetic changes are reversible and do not change your DNA sequence, but they can change how your body reads a DNA sequence.[85]

There are different types of ways that epigenetic changes affect gene expressions like DNA methylation, histone modification, or noncoding RNA. Much of this is beyond any of us. But it is intriguing that there are scientists and researchers who study genomics who have determined that what we experience—our stories—can interact with our bodies and minds at a cellular level. Not only this, these changes can then be passed down to our children and their children, effectively altering the way that the fibers of our bodies are woven over generations.

In other words, according to folks at Harvard University, now there is no "nature or nurture" question.[86] It's undoubtedly both. Furthermore, "stressful environmental conditions may leave an imprint on the epigenome that is passed down to future generations."[87]

So, what does this mean when our nature and nurture are touched by trauma? What does it mean for our healing, and what does it mean for our future if we want to stop the cycle and heal beyond the limiting confines of our family's tree?

Dr. Anita Phillips, a psychologist and trauma specialist notes in an interview on the *Made for This* podcast with Jennie Allen about the COVID-19 pandemic:

> There's so much unknown that this is a bona fide trauma. Our nervous systems, as a result, are activated in the presence of this anxiety and uncertainty and fear. When our nervous system is activated in that way, it begins to kind of pull on our body. So, people may not only be feeling emotions like anxiety, fear, sadness, but also physical fatigue, digestive problems, racing heart, shortness of breath, even when they're not exerting themselves. You might think, "what is wrong with me?" Your body is perfectly aware of what's going on. Even if in your mind, you're trying to tell yourself that it's nothing.[88]

I've been wondering: how is this period in history, the one we are breathing in right now (the one where the next generation has been affectionately termed the "Doomer Generation"), going to impact my children and their children (assuming, you know, all's well by then on, ahem, Earth)? And what does this have to do with our lives or recovery today? Or the lives of those we care about and feed breakfast to every day?

While all of this sounds pretty bleak (and in many ways is), there is some good news. All throughout history, we learn of people who rise from the ashes to live new lives. Healed lives. In scripture, too, God points to people who are affected by their family lineages, by sin and brokenness, yet are also redeemed from them. There are also other parts of scripture found in Exodus and Ezekiel that paint very different pictures of a loving God. In one key passage, scripture recognizes that children will be impacted by the sins and trauma of their family members. In another, it talks about a God who brings freedom for the offspring of the afflicted. So our kids still have a chance.

In my experience, both are true (classic God: bringing truth from all angles). I have lived with the consequences of a broken and hurting world—and a broken and hurting mother. Consequences like these drove me to escape and seek out love in all the wrong places (as the country song goes) with all the wrong misters. But I have also been freed from the bonds of my own gnarly family tree.

The good news is that *we have the ability to take action; we have choices to make.* We don't necessarily have to repeat the same mistakes and relive the same trauma as our families. Though trauma can impact our lives down to the cellular level, we don't have to stay stuck living unhealthy patterns. The living rhythms we've been pointing to throughout this book can help us get there—to a place of freedom. We are not our trauma.

While taking the first step toward healing might not be easy, or might not seem like a real choice before us, it is possible. I can testify to that. In this moment, we can let go of the unlovely and have compassion for our stories. We can set our monsters down, open our hands and hearts, and surrender.

Chapter 16

From Silence to Story

I must consciously work at reviewing both the progress of the ache and the progress of the healing.
—Philip Yancey, *Reaching for the Invisible God*

For the longest time, I didn't have a voice. I mean, I had one—don't get me wrong, I could sing in the shower like your average angsty momma, but in everyday interactions, I never shared my thoughts or opinions. Especially if it had anything to do with myself or my body or boundaries. Those who have experienced trauma that violates the body know that sharing opinions—vocalizing boundaries—is a skill we lost, or never developed, and we have to *learn* how to do it. We have to learn how to find our voices again. It takes practice.

For example, I was driving and a song came on the radio. Isn't it strange how songs can bring us back to different points in time with such amazing and raw clarity? In this particular song, the artist on the Christian station was singing, "He is jealous for me. Loves like a hurricane. I am a tree, bending beneath the weight of his wind and mercy."

"How He Loves" is one of the songs that cut through some of the rubble and rubbish in my mind. Moreover, songs like this one gave me the words that I longed to speak—words about hope, love, courage, and identity—to those around me, especially women. The author of the song, John Mark McMillan, could say what I wanted to say but did not have the words or the confidence to.

When I lived in Michigan in my early to midtwenties, I had my first "small group" Bible study experience. It was utterly terrifying to me on all sorts of levels (and I talk about this in more detail in another book, *Downstairs Church*), but basically it was this: Girl (me): broken: beyond: repair: seeks: Jesus: and fellowship: and healing: but: can't: talk.

I mean, I could talk, but it was almost impossible to get anything of substance out. I couldn't share what was in my heart: my thoughts, dreams, doubts, struggles, past. I sat there like a garden statue, chewing my Nicorette and trying to give myself little pep talks.

Now—talk now.

(Silent pause.)

Okay, you missed your chance now but wait . . . after they share about red lipstick and stomach stapling and cool aunt hacks . . .

(Silent pause.)

Darn, you missed it again.

So, during one of the last meetings we had for that calendar year, I brought a CD missing its cover and sat down in my usual spot on the floor in the living room of Lisa, the leader/cool aunt type who hosted the group in her home. I set the CD on top of a decorative pillow but didn't say a word. I could sense that the other women wondered why my awkward self came in with a CD and no explanation. At a ladies' small group, there is *always* an explanation for stuff.

Finally, one of the women asked, "Caroline, did you bring something?"

I nodded and handed her this CD and tried to explain. "I—um—I really connected with this song. I thought—I was thinking maybe some of you—I mean I connected with this song . . . and wanted to share it with you."

Lisa was gracious and took the CD and put it into the CD player (long before the era of streaming music), and it began. I stared at my feet, cross-legged. As the music began, I looked up a little but didn't want anyone to see me look at them.

Did they feel it too?

Was the artist able to convey to the women in the small circle sitting cross-legged on the floor with our teas and coffees and study Bibles (either worn and highlighted like Lisa's or brand new like mine) that God loves us?

Ridiculously.

Passionately.

Persistently.

Jealously.

Could they feel me saying those words to them with my eyes and proclaiming the good news?

OMG! Sisters, God loves us and cherishes us and longs for us and no matter our lives or brokenness or messiness or addiction or trauma or shame or silence, we are wholly and completely, beautifully and amazingly loved! We are more than our pasts, more than our traumas, more than our brokenness.

I'm not sure the effect of the song on the other women in the room, but it continued to move me. I didn't realize it at the time, but I wanted to testify. I wanted to share with these women about my pain and suffering and about how God had delivered me and was delivering me, despite my fear and silence and shame. This is what my voice needed to do, but I couldn't say the words myself, so I spoke them through someone else's song.

What I also didn't realize at the time was the story behind the song. Before composing the song, John Mark McMillan experienced the tremendous and sudden loss of a young friend, and his grief, anger at God, and honest doubts created a space where his vulnerability led him to a new place of surrender and ultimately healing. John Mark shared:

> In church we like to pretend everything's okay a lot. And most of the songs we sing in church are sort of the happy songs, but only 15 to 20 percent of the songs found in the Bible are happy. The other 75 to 80 percent are the angry ones, the sad ones, or the brutally honest ones. For me, the song was not about "how much" he loves us: "he loves us so much that he died." It was "how" he loves us, "the way" he loves us. He loves us in ways that are not like we think; they're better than we think.[89]

Through his pain, struggle, and indeed trauma, John Mark experienced healing because he came to have an honest conversation with God, an honest struggle. The trial he experienced did not lead him away from God, but closer. He didn't have to pretend to have faith or trust that even the death of his friend was going to work out for his good in the end. He did not have to fake acceptance. He came real, broken, and carrying his own monsters, and God met him in that place, was close to him, and showed him the truth of and extent of his love.

> How have you experienced your own version of a reckoning with God? How have you been able to bring your honest feelings and struggle to God—or even to a close friend?

Over the years, if someone looked at my life, say on my Facebook timeline or IG grid, they might see the progression of a woman who moved from silence to story. Or you might see a woman who still likes to throw a good Christine Caine quote out there from time to time. Because, let's face it, some people are really good at telling it like it is (plus, it sounds better in an Australian accent). Maybe this is why social media and memes are so popular. We don't have to say it; someone else can. All we have to do is share.

C. S. Lewis said, "Isn't it funny how day by day nothing changes, but when you look back everything is different."[90]

Today, I can share, I do have a voice, even though sometimes it is still challenging to use it. Sometimes, I still have to psych myself up, like when I gave myself pep talks in Lisa's living room. This is especially true if we are talking about trauma and giving voice to the things that are easier to keep buried, though they keep us sick. "We are only as sick as our secrets," my friends in twelve-step recovery say.

Have you experienced the freedom to give voice to your experience? In having and using your voice? It is freeing when we realize we aren't singing alone.

> What do you need to vocalize right now?

In her book, *This Here Flesh*, Cole Arthur Riley talks about her own experience growing up as a Black woman and how her family history impacted and impacts her own story today. She says, "Sometimes you can't talk someone into believing their dignity. You do what you can to make a person feel unashamed of themselves, and you hope in time they'll believe in their beauty all on their own."[91] For her, story is a powerful tool that sheds light on intergenerational experience. When shared, our stories can open a door to believing in beauty. The beauty in the mess and heartache, the beauty of our stories, the beauty of ourselves.

Have you had the opportunity to share your story or pieces of it? Are you ready to step into the fullness of what transparency can bring? Are you ready to move from silence to story?

Cherry-Picking

Trauma, including things from my childhood and things that happened to me because of my addiction to alcohol and other drugs, changed me. It solidified the gross misconceptions or lies that I came to believe about myself. Thoughts like *I am dirty, broken, and unlovable* consumed me. It caused me to be led by fear and not love. To love was something to be feared because, from my experience, vulnerability only created more pain.

Yet, while the sting of the events of my young life caused immense hurt, trauma also opened a door to redemption, healing, and freedom.

One of my favorite verses of scripture, and a favorite of so many others, is Jeremiah 29:11. "For I know the plans I have for you, declares the LORD, plans to prosper you and not to harm you, plans to give you hope and a future."

A very well-meaning Christian counselor years ago gave me this verse on a piece of white paper. In my early twenties, I started therapy (again) because I could not figure out why I kept doing things that weren't in line with what I wanted to do or in line with my values. At the time, I did not understand how much past trauma impacted my day-to-day life, relationships, and choices. Why I still lived in silence with closed fists.

While I connect with this verse now, at the time the words tasted bitter. It read like a platitude, something painted on faux barnwood in suburban kitchens. It was not something my heart connected with. It looked good on paper; but in truth, in the everyday grit of my human experience, it felt too good to be true. Surviving two sexual assaults, one in high school and one later in college, led me into a dark season (almost a couple decades long) of deep shame and despair. I knew nothing of hope or a future. I did not think I would live past thirty years of age.

Jeremiah 29:11 was spoken to people amid hardship and suffering: Jews who had been living under enemies and then brought into exile from Jerusalem to Babylon. These were likely people who wanted immediate salvation. Rescue. Jeremiah tells the people that they've got some time to wait (like seventy years) in captivity, but that hope is coming. In a beautifully merciful way, God promises that although the current thorn might not go away—they can be certain that there is a plan and a future and a hope for them.

Now, I'm as guilty of cherry-picking encouraging verses as the next person, but when I look deeper, sometimes God reveals just how upside down—yet miraculous—God's ways are. While God's people might have wanted immediate rescue, there were other plans.

Getting rid of the remnants of my traumatic past and breaking free from the chains of addiction have been more than challenging. It has taken me years to get to a place where I can speak about some of my experiences without my face flushing crimson. It's taken much longer than I would have liked to start to see myself as a woman with dignity and confidence and self-respect. Like the Jews from the Old Testament, my captivity lingered.

When the counselor handed me the verse, I remember feeling so alone. I thought there was no way she understood what I had been through.

At the time, I struggled to share my story with anyone. No one knew about my journey through addiction, despair, obsession, and sin—not even my close family knew all the gritty details. So when I sat down with this strange woman, I was afraid. I was so ashamed of my sexual past that I thought the counselor might run as fast as she could in the opposite direction of her office or lock me out. I worried that my muddied past and list of adverse childhood experiences (ACEs) might scare her away. I wondered if she had ever worked with a woman who suffered repeated sexual assault, was drowning in addiction, and was so broken.

After reading aloud the verse from Jeremiah, and after my crying for some time, she asked me to tell my story, which was an invitation to use my voice.

I recall sitting in her chair, feeling the scratchy material of the armrests, smelling a gentle waft of vanilla from a nearby candle. I took a sip of water and began. I told her about how my drinking and drug use took off in high school. I told her about being at a party and being vulnerable to the attack. I shared with her how I lost any feeling of agency or control over my own body—things spiraling from there.

She did not get up or run away. She listened, her lips pressed into a closed smile. Her eyes welled with tears that she tried to hide. I sensed compassion, even though I knew her own experience growing up had likely been much safer. Softer. Kinder to her.

I am not alone. My story is not unique. There are countless women, men, and all folks with longer lists of experiences that make it a miracle they are standing today. Many women—too many women—know my pain. Not to mention the pain of intergenerational trauma that I've touched on (genocide, racial trauma, the list continues).

Jeremiah knew struggle too. He despaired over the world he lived in with its hardships and sin—just like we do today. Just like women with trauma histories, women like me, often look at the world with sadness, and try to wade through the mess and hopelessness. Yet God spoke a word to him. A word about hope. And future. And possibility. A word that God wanted Jeremiah to share. Though he suffered and witnessed horrific suffering, the posture of Jeremiah's heart remained open to give and receive.

Connection

One of the incredible things about being a woman in recovery today is that we know we are not alone. Though our stories are not unique, they have immeasurable value. Our stories can also be shared so that others know they are not alone. We may not understand why things happen to us and in the world around us, but we can take comfort in the fact that our traumatic stories can be redeemed into stories of hope and salvation.

But how do we get there? How can we move from silence to story?

I wish I had a simple solution for you. I wish I could say there was one thing to do or say that would help move you into a place of compassion for your story and ultimate purpose. A quick fix.

What I can share from my personal experience, from the countless people I've worked with and from my mother, is that healing is a process. It is a journey. It can be a choice. And perhaps most importantly, you have the choice today.

Along with the other rhythms outlined in this book, we can also live open-handed when we ask others to join us. For some of us, that might also mean inviting God in. For some of us, the spiritual still carries with it too much religious trauma and baggage, and that's okay too. As we say in recovery, "Keep coming back."

There has never been a church sanctuary or conference room or stage where I've told my story or talked about recovery where I didn't come with a posture of utter surrender. Any introvert will know what I mean. Coming to share my story (whether on a stage or in a book or even on social media) is an act of courage, and I need help to do this. We need help to use our voices. On our own, we may not have the strength, but in community, when connected to others and maybe even to God, anything is possible.

In the rooms of recovery meetings or other types of support groups like divorce or grief support groups, there is usually a circle of chairs (one of my favorite phrases, if you didn't know by now). It is a visual reminder that we aren't alone. We can have, if we choose, a circle of support around us as we go to the deep places, the hard places in our stories. We don't have to be alone as we move toward healing.

With open hands—together—we can learn to move on from those things that haunt our family trees by breaking the silence and letting go of shame. We can move from silence to story in a way that breaks bonds and brings freedom. We can, like Jeremiah, rise above suffering by setting our sights on hope. We can take action to disrupt the cycle and wait to see what happens when we are ready to step into the new.

Interlude 4

Take Back the Night

I walk with the others, men, women, and all folks, up to the state capitol building and make my way to the top of the steps where the speakers are gathered. I take one last bite of the sandwich I bought at one of the coffee shops I love and smile to myself. It feels good to taste salt on my tongue.

I've practiced my talk again and again, crying into the living room mirror. Laughing into it. Standing tall. It's one thing to do this in secret. It's another to share my story out loud.

As my turn approaches, I look around the crowd. It is a diverse group, students of all ages. Some hold signs that say, "Take Back the Night."

They are passionate.

It's my turn now.

I face the crowd and clutch the microphone with my sweaty hand. The papers in my other hand flutter with the wind. My voice starts in a whisper.

Quiet.

Louder.

Louder.

Louder as I slowly say the words that for years have strangled me.

The crowd is silent like the night.

I share my poem, "She Raged":

She raged that he hurt her so terribly and then pretended it didn't happen. She raged because the other kids she knew seemed to be so happy. She raged because she couldn't scream. She raged because she felt smaller and smaller, until she didn't want to be seen. She raged because she had tried so hard to die but couldn't. She raged because the world was so beautiful, and she couldn't really see it. She raged because she didn't trust that anyone could ever love her. She raged because the rules kept changing, and she didn't know what they were. She raged that there were rules. She raged because she learned to live numb, so she wouldn't feel anything. She raged because she never knew joy. She raged because nobody knew who she really was, as she tried to be who they wanted in order to be loved and accepted. She raged because she married people she never wanted. She raged because she was so ashamed of her divorces. She raged because she let others hold her down. She raged because looking at the tiny faces of her children made her remember. She raged because she had to remember. She raged because she couldn't remember. She raged because she did remember. She raged that it took her so long to tell. She raged because some people didn't believe her memories. She raged that it took her body years to untie the tight knots that bound it. She raged that it took her so long to trust herself. She raged because her violated body struggled just to survive. She raged because she never believed how beautiful she was. She raged that she tried to live the kind of life she was "supposed to," when all she really wanted was to sing and dance in the wind. She raged that she had so many rules of perfection for herself, and she could never keep them. She raged that she could never commit. She raged that what she was struggling to commit to, she never wanted. She raged that she felt different. She raged that she was different and couldn't let others know, for fear she wouldn't be accepted. The rage built up in her, until she was overtaken by it and transformed. The rage became something beautiful. Broken became purpose.

The clapping begins.

Quiet.

Loud.

Louder.

I float off the stage.

I feel heard.

Understood.

I find my voice.

—Mother

Chapter 17

Rhythms of Disruption

There comes a moment when people who have been dabbling in religion ("Man's Search for God!") suddenly draw back. Supposing we really found him? We never meant it to come to that! Worse still, supposing he had found us?

—C. S. Lewis, *Miracles*

The good news is this: there is a way out.

In Romans 8:28, Paul says, "And we know that in all things God works for the good of those who love him, who have been called according to his purpose."

If you struggle with this thought as I have (I will gladly—yet begrudgingly—admit this), that's okay. I think sometimes as believers or not-surers, there are hard theological and gritty truths that sound pretty profound and sparkly and like something on a magnet you'd find inspirational on your fridge. It sounds great, but the reality is, *truth is hard*. This is a challenging thing to contemplate when we've been through really hard things.

Our agonies have a purpose; while I've struggled with this thought, in my own life I've found value in moving beyond my doubt. We might not see it now and we might not ever fully understand, but we can rest assured that God has a plan for how we can overcome. God can craft a masterpiece like a child makes art from nothing: a handful of dandelions, watercolor on paper cups, a collection of twigs and leaves and moss, a mound of dirt as self-portrait. We can find purpose in our pain.

Check out how Paul continues several verses later:

> Who shall separate us from the love of Christ? Shall trouble or hardship or persecution or famine or nakedness or danger or sword? As it is written:
>
>> "For your sake we face death all day long; we are considered as sheep to be slaughtered."
>
> No, in all these things we are more than conquerors through him who loved us. For I am convinced that neither death nor life, neither angels nor demons, neither the present nor the future, nor any powers, neither height nor depth, nor anything else in all creation, will be able to separate us from the love of God that is in Christ Jesus our Lord. (Romans 8:35–39)

The Apostle Paul doubles down here. We can choose to read this passage to mean that all our trials and tribulations—the excruciating, crucifying stuff, the adverse childhood haunts and traumas and agonies like icebergs, only a small part visible above the surface—all of this can be for our ultimate good.

My hope for you right now is that you believe this, but I know my limitations. And I know the limitations of language. And I know that many of us have experienced hurts from the church; the thought of reading scripture or listening to any of it is more than tough. And I know that for me, it took a lot more than reading it or someone telling me this was the way it was. I had to experience it. I had to get to a place of looking back and seeing how my life made sense when the pieces were finally put into place, one giant muddled puzzle that gets clearer the farther away you are standing from it.

With Vision

When I first met Claudia, she was rocking on a twin bed, wrapped in a donated quilt, looking toward the large bay window of a dining room converted into a five-person bedroom in a women's sober living home. She had faded red hair (once purple, she'd say) with dark roots and clothes that hung off her frame like an oversized sweater in the closet. I asked if I could sit down.

"Hi, I'm Caroline."

"Hi, Caroline."

Claudia went blind two weeks before we met from overuse of methamphetamines. Did you know that too much of this drug can cause a film to develop over the eyes like glaucoma? Meth use can cause damage to the small blood vessels in the retina, leading to a condition called methamphetamine-associated retinopathy.

I told Claudia a bit about my recovery story and asked her about her story. I wasn't prepared for what she was about to tell me and almost hesitate to relay it here for fear that it might bring your own ghosts back for a visit. This is your trigger warning.

Claudia was impregnated twice—by her father. Also, Claudia never met her mother until at ten years old she was asked to identify the body in the morgue.

"It was cold," she said. "I didn't want to meet her like that."

She went on without tears, recounting trauma after trauma after trauma. Then, she got to the sexual assault in the homeless shelter that led her to this home in East Tennessee, where I had the opportunity to sit on the edge of her bed and hear her secrets like a best friend from middle school.

What led her to finally break down, tears falling from her cloudy eyes:

"Sometimes I wonder if I met her, my mother, if my life would have turned out like this. Sometimes I see—used to see—women with their mothers, little girls with their mothers, and get so sad. Why couldn't I have that kind of love? Why couldn't I have had a mother?"

I broke down too, though she couldn't see. Or maybe she did.

It was a good question. *The* question. But what followed next took me by surprise. "Surprise" not being a strong enough word to capture awe.

Claudia began to talk to me about her faith and about how she knew the Lord was always near. Even though all these things had happened to her, things I could only imagine or try not to imagine, she still said that she believed her God would continue to be there for her.

"It's been my faith that's carried me through."

Then she asked me to pray with her. I asked her what she wanted me to pray for and she said, "Can you ask God to help me see?"

Even Claudia, with all she'd been through, had faith that her traumas and lack of a mother's presence was something she could find her way through. Her vision inspired.

Foggy Faith

One Sunday morning, I drove to church listening to Christian rock music in my favorite button-up denim shirt.* I was think-ing about my mom, like I have a tendency to do, wondering how she was, what she was up to, hoping above all hope that she was still single and hadn't met "the one" again.

I pulled into the parking lot, finding a spot farthest from the entrance but easiest to get the heck out of there after the benediction to avoid traffic, and was about to walk into church alone like I usually did. Though it was getting easier, this was still tough, like walking under water. It required prayer. Walk-ing in, not wanting to be noticed, trying to find a seat that's not too close to the front but not the last row either. Strangers so close I could smell men's aftershave. Let me tell you, for women like me, it can be exhausting just figuring out where to sit in a crowd that feels safe. In case you didn't know: people in recov-ery usually have a well-thought-out exit strategy.

Not being able to control my immediate environment (trauma symptoms resurfacing) made attending church regu-larly near impossible, but I still showed up.

The service began like it usually did, and I was able to feel a bit more comfortable as the lights dimmed. Sometimes I had anxiety attacks that came out of nowhere (I have the name for them now), my heart racing and hands sweaty cold. But on this particular Sunday, I wasn't sure if it was the drive or the music or the way the light hit just so, but I felt a bit calmer than usual and a bit more comfortable. The first couple songs ended, then

---

* As an aside, my husband detests Christian rock music, but we still make it work.

the announcements, and then the pastor, a middle-aged man with graying hair wearing blue jeans (thankfully, not of the "skinny" variety), began to speak.

He started with a story, as most pastors do. The story began with a woman who had been sexually abused.

I'm not sure about all of what he said, I'd float in and out of hearing about the pain she felt and the betrayal. Hands on skin. About how she always questioned the existence of God because *how could a loving God exist if this could happen to her?*

It felt like the story was directed right at me. Like when you are at a concert and you are sure that the lead singer is winking at you.

"God was there," he said, "the whole time. He was standing in the doorway, by the side of the bed. He was holding your hand through it all. Jesus wept."

He looked up and I swear he made eye contact with me, at least that's how it felt. I knew that God was speaking through this story on this particular Sunday to reach a particular place inside me that was still hiding in a dark corner. A little girl shaking.

The tears rolled down my cheeks, and my chest heaved with sobs. I don't know how the people around me perceived what was happening. In the past, I would have been super self-conscious, but at that moment I felt okay taking up space. That day I came to believe with my whole heart that God was there when it happened—when all of it happened. And I started to feel safe, at home, in my own body.

Like Claudia, this was my moment of hope, of faith, a glimmer in the darkness.

God was there.

In the hundreds of millions or billions of people who experience trauma in all its varying forms. The military veteran or the abuse survivor. The refugee or the migrant worker. Claudia. My mom or me.

God is there.

Here.

The world might be a broken place, but God is still just and loving and can feel our struggle and humanity in the very core of God's presence. God upholds the struggle of women—and men, all folks—alike.

This was comforting to me in a way that I had never experienced before. The sermon I heard that Sunday morning was exactly what I needed to hear, exactly when I needed to hear it. And interestingly, after this, my view of church started to shift too. If I was loved and held and cared for despite my own brokenness and past experiences, others were too. I did not have to let my resentment or bitterness choke out what was trying to grow around me in those walls that had once felt so suffocating and unsafe. It was okay to start letting people know me, even if I was still not sure, even if it was hard.

At that moment, I knew it was time to break out of the isolation and pain. A butterfly emerging from the sticky shell of a pupa. When I started to let others in, let God in, the darkness that surrounded me through years of substance use started to vanish. I knew I was being given a new opportunity to heal. An opportunity to ask, seek, and knock, grateful for the door to knock on, to trust that God was there. An opportunity to hold my story with compassion.

Lore Ferguson Wilbert says in *The Understory*:

> ... the work of being here and not there or not yet there
> is good work. It is courageous work. It is hard work.
> And it is not death work. It is resurrection work. It is
> the work of remembering what it means to be "mag-
> nificently oneself."

We can hold our stories with compassion and begin to feel
at home, once again, in our bodies.

The rhythms of disrupting trauma and clearing the way for
healing outlined in this book are precious gifts. We are given
the grace and the tools we need to heal.

When we *Protect the Temple*, we are invited to view—and
treat—ourselves as the lovely humans we are, regardless of
what we have lived through or done.

As we *Practice Forgiveness*, we open up to experience the
freedom that letting go of hurt or anger can bring. We are able
to move into a place of compassion and empathy for those
who may have harmed us, even ourselves.

By taking action to *Lean In to the Struggle*, we are able to see
our lives in light of a bigger picture, one that involves embrac-
ing all our stories.

When we *Get Real* with ourselves and others, the destructive illusion of shame is broken.

And finally, as we *Let God*, we can surrender with an outstretched soul and receive the love we have desperately longed
for.

Wherever you are in your journey and whatever your pathway, know this: your journey is beautiful. You are traveling
your path for a reason. Your ancestors traveled their paths for a

reason too. You are, sweet friend, reading these words for a reason—at this very moment in time. Maybe it's time for you to be alive again. Maybe it's time to let something new happen with your old mess. Maybe your family tree has new shoots sprouting near the trunk. New life. New opportunity. Maybe your kids don't have to repeat your past. Maybe what you are seeking, you already have.

I wish I could say that I am always here. And by "here," I mean always healed enough that my past trauma symptoms don't come back ringing the dusty doorbell. Always *with vision*: having compassion for my experience, confidence in my purpose and trust that God really does work all things out for our good.

But I'm going to be real with you. Sometimes it comes back, a little, like a bump in the grass or a hole where some small creature has burrowed. Trauma symptoms can resurface. We have to keep working. I've experienced it. Women I work with or speak to have lived it. But this is also real: the mountain of trauma can be moved. We can uproot trauma and live free.

Even if doubt creeps in, even if it's hard to have faith, even if we are reminded of the trauma we've experienced, even if we take more than two steps back: we can "trust that, out beyond the perimeter of fog, God still reigns and has not abandoned us, no matter how it may appear."[92] Sometimes understanding and healing take time.

Five Actions You Can Take: Let God

- Make a dream/inspiration/vision board centered on this question: What does it look like to live open-handed or vulnerable once again?

- Share your story (or part of it) with a trusted friend, small group, or recovery space. Then, journal about how it feels to share it.
- Try a resilience practice (see the appendix in the back of this book). This can be especially helpful if you find that sharing your story brings up some things that still need more healing.
- Reach out for more support from a counselor, therapist, substance use counselor, recovery coach, or someone else if you think you are ready to take your healing to the next level (or if you feel moved to after reading).
- Finish this journal prompt:

  When I am surrendered, I can . . .
  "When I am free, I will . . ."

Interlude 5

Free

I sit on the open front porch of the farmhouse and look again at the beautiful gardens that I helped to plant. I think of the many hours that my sisters and I spend there, watering the flowers and shrubs and pulling the weeds that spring up after long rains.

I love the smell of the garden after the rain, as it smells earthy and fresh.

It is an endless process, digging hole after hole in the black, rich soil. Finding the perfect home for each flower. And if the sunlight isn't right or they don't bloom or grow well, they are moved to another spot to thrive. Each year boasts a different garden, a surprise of color.

I love the cycle: the work, the planting, the beauty.

I walk slowly to the side of the house, where stepping stones lead to an arched trellis covered with blooming purple clematis.

Take a deep breath.

Sometimes it feels good to stop and appreciate what I've done. What we've done.

It is right before sunset and it is magical. Each part of the garden glows with fiery light, first yellow, then orange, then pink, each in its own time. The flowers, too, take their turns bowing and turning color under the new palette in the sky. A myriad of connecting colors. A prism of light. The sweet smell of farm, of home, fills the air.

It's so different now. Different from when I was a girl. I'm different. I'm new.

It is during these final moments of the day that I'm reminded of beauty. Dirt under my nails, reminding me that I am alive.

Conclusion

Grace Does

I've always been enamored by trees. Their sturdiness and majesty. The way clapping leaves sound like ocean waves.

Trees have witnessed some of the most profound moments of my life. My first beer at eleven under the shade of a wrinkly oak. Waves of tears as a teen near rows of sapling pine. Unfinished stories and screenplays that I wrote with them as my mysterious muses and backrests, their branches my only readers. They've stood by as my silent smoking buddies and held me up when I needed a place to pee outside. In early recovery, they waved to me as I ascended sand dunes and pranced through quaking aspen and sugar maple groves with my best friend and puppy, Mo.

Trees may have a place in your life, your past, too.

Beronda Montgomery, a former professor of biochemistry and molecular biology at Michigan State University, wrote an article called "Trees Don't Rush to Heal from Trauma and Neither Should We." In it she states:

> Trees notice when there is damage or loss, and embark upon a process of recuperation and healing. They don't

just ignore trauma or aging in order to get back to business as usual. Indeed, failure to respond—and respond actively and dynamically—could result in long-term poor health, even death. So, when a wound occurs, trees initiate a protective response that often takes place in two distinct stages—an initial, rapid chemical phase, followed by a slower, long-term physical adaptation. [. . .]

Covering a wound prematurely simply to keep the damage out of sight, without attention to openly dealing with it through cleansing and therapeutic care, can lead to a festering of issues rather than a healthy progression toward healing, reformulation, growth and thriving.[93]

Trees tell us something about healing and the need to respond to trauma. They also show how different approaches are needed. A response in the short term and a strategy for the long game.

There are tools and practical ways to disrupt cycles of intergenerational trauma. There are things that have helped my own journey (and help on the daily) like Protecting the Temple, Practicing Forgiveness, Leaning into the Struggle, Getting Real, and last but not least, Letting God.

Just as there is a season for everything (*turn, turn, turn*), there is also a choice nestled within what Montgomery calls a "delicate balancing act in the struggle to recover from trauma." There is a time to apply the salve, to heal the wound.

There is also a time to grow a new branch, even plant a seed: to allow love back into our lives or perhaps into our lives for the first time.

Grace can be a sudden summer rain shower, or it can be slow and drip like the pine sap that crystallizes on a towering, lone evergreen. Sometimes it takes a while to be able to feel and know we are lovable. It can take work. Like I share with folks who are celebrating a recovery milestone: recovery and healing are not easy, but the work is always worth it. And so are you.

You are worth every second of the work.

You deserve to be free of anything that has been preventing you from knowing your true worth and knowing the One who loves you. You deserve to experience a grace that glistens. You deserve to "know a new freedom and a new happiness," as my recovery friends say.[94]

Our lives may have started on the wrong side of things, in places of despair and captivity, but now (praise God) we can commit to a new path. Trauma doesn't have to have the last word. Grace does.

And I am so grateful, so grateful, so grateful.

The tears tickle my eyelashes.

My face flushes with thanks.

We can be both pummeled and lifted up in this life.

To the person that is questioning their past/future/worth/purpose/possibility today, I'd like to say this:

You are loved.
You are lovely.
You can mother.
You can be mothered.
You can love.
You can fight.

You can disrupt the cycle.
You are precious.
You belong to God.
You are altogether beautiful, my darling; there is no flaw in you.*
There is hope.

This January, I'll be celebrating (God willing) another year living in recovery. I have a loving family of my own. I have a roof over my head and a safe and warm place to sleep. We have more food than we need. Today, I have healed relationships with my extended family, and I pay my bills on time. I get to work with other women in recovery and share my story. I even started an online storytelling platform for women in addiction, trauma, and mental health recovery called Circle of Chairs. Today, I can say with boldness and awe that I am a woman in recovery. I am a woman with hope.

My mother is too.

We know that according to Romans 5:5, "... hope does not put us to shame, because God's love has been poured out into our hearts through the Holy Spirit, who has been given to us." And we can accept this love. We can receive this love. Even women like me who have lived in the dust of shame can embrace what G. K. Chesterton has called the "furious love of God," a tremendous hope.

My story, and that of my mother's, has been an uphill climb, with steep and treacherous summits. You have your own story too. Mountains and valleys and riverbeds that speak of the unspeakable. Yet, at the same time, we can point to overflowing waterfalls that remind us that no matter what, we can

---

* Song of Songs 4:7

keep moving. We can be a part of the birth of resilience in our lives. And, importantly, for the next generation.

Our hearts can be opened to the transforming power of love and to the amazing truth that God does have a plan. He does have a future. He does have hope for us. It doesn't matter our past chains or our past trauma or our momma's trauma; what does matter is that every new day is an opportunity to choose hope.

Those of us whose trees have fallen (in all senses of the word) will be given the opportunity to grow anew. Not in spite of the trauma but because of it. Not because we haven't experienced struggle, but because we have.

I love how author Cole Arthur Riley puts it in *This Here Flesh*:

> For every second that our organs and bones sustain us is a miracle. When those bones heal, when our wounds scab over, this is our call to marvel at our bodies—their regeneration, their stability or frailty. This grows our sense of dignity.[95]

Sweet friend, I hope you've made it to the good part in your story where you realize your life has beauty and dignity. You are standing on your past and look down and see a tiny green shoot coming up from between your feet. You hear God's promise to you: all things will be made new. You "will be like a tree planted by the water that sends out its roots by the stream" (Jeremiah 17:8).

Grave Dancing

Today is that day.

I get out of my car, looking at the grave in front of me. No, you cannot hold me down any longer. I take off my shoes, feeling the soft earth beneath my feet. It has taken years to get to this point, but I am ready now. I kneel down, giving thanks for the ruddy ground. Earth is real in my grasp. Forehead to the dirt, arms outstretched.

I rise, arms reaching to the sky, holding the posture longer than I think I can.

I turn, facing the sun. I laugh in the light, then begin to twirl, whirling faster and faster.

As I gain momentum, my joy increases. The trees are my audience, cheering.

I dance on the grave of the one who kept me powerless. The child in me rejoices, the woman sings, as she reaches new heights. No one can stop us now.

And the dance becomes our life, shedding everything that once held us in its grip. And the darkness that once surrounded us so completely gives way to the light of sunrise.

We reclaim the body that is ours and the voices that for so long were silent.

We reclaim our spirit, that deadened part that is now alive.

Sound erupts from within us, feeling bursts forth. We rejoice that our stories are heard. We reach for the others. We dance with life.

—Mother

Appendix

Resilience Practices

No feeling is final.

—Rainer Maria Rilke

For those of us who have experienced these things, talking about trauma can elicit some of the very symptoms I am describing here. Maybe in reading, sometimes your breath is quickening, your fingers or toes feeling tingly. Maybe you've tuned out completely and skipped on to the next section or even put this book down because it's too much. Maybe you started to have flashbacks of an experience you'd rather forget or maybe something is coming up that you didn't know was buried somewhere deep below the surface, like one of those fish that can live on the bottom of the ocean floor in such high pressure.

However you are showing up, I'd like to guide you through a series of resilience practices that are inspired by some of those found in Seeking Safety that you might find helpful (I do). The goal of these practices is to shift our focus to the present and to promote resilience. There have been studies on both the science and spirituality behind the effectiveness of these practices, and if you need a respite from what may be coming up for you, I hope you can meet me here.

Resilience Practice #1: Get Moving

Trauma causes havoc with your body—adding stress and all sorts of overloads of chemicals found in your body, like cortisol. Over time, an increase in "hyperarousal," or a constant state of fear for your body, can be harmful for your health.

Movement or exercise helps you to expend excess adrenaline caused by hyperarousal and also releases endorphins, which is your body's own feel-good sauce. Movement and exercise can actually repair harm that has been done to your nervous system and help you to stay in the present. Here are a couple suggestions for getting moving:

- **Try to exercise for thirty minutes or more on most days.** You can also do ten-minute spurts of exercise throughout the day as well.

- **Do rhythmic exercise.** Exercise that is rhythmic is great for your mind and is healthy as it moves different parts of your body, including your arms and legs. Rhythmic exercises include walking or running, dancing, swimming, aerobic classes, HIIT (high intensity interval training) workouts, and group activities like basketball or volleyball.

- **Add a mindfulness element.** Focusing on your breathing can help to relax you during activity as well. Rock climbing, boxing, weight training, or yoga are all examples of mindful activities that connect your body with your mind.

Resilience Practice #2: Self-Regulate Your Nervous System

One of the most life-changing things I learned about my trauma symptoms and how to lean in to my struggle was that there are things that I can do to help my body and mind self-regulate. No matter what my anxiety level is, I can work to calm and soothe myself.

What Does Trauma Do to the Nervous System?

Trauma can impact us in many ways: physically, emotionally, and spiritually. Researchers have found out some interesting ways that trauma changes us. I won't get in to the super scientific information; basically, trauma propels the body and our nervous system into a state that causes us to be unable to self-regulate. In other words, when we are in a trauma response of any duration, we are in overdrive.

Our system, in particular our nervous system, gets stuck in the "on" position and leads us to be overstimulated, unable to calm, and always in a state of "fight or flight" or near it.

You may be able to relate with being overwhelmed by anxiety, anger, restlessness, panic, and hyperactivity. These symptoms can all be present after being triggered by a traumatic event. Even years later.

During a traumatic event, the body, which includes the brain, tries to protect itself. The body and brain actually shut down all nonessential processes and get stuck in survival mode. This is when the sympathetic nervous system increases stress hormones and prepares the body to fight, flee, or freeze.

What Is Self-Regulation?

Ultimately, the mind and body go through more than a lot. So how can we relearn or retrain our bodies to self-regulate?

Self-regulation (in the non-sciencey way to talk about it) is the practice of loving self-control. We can find and learn ways to calm and even change the arousal system in our bodies that is responsible for trauma responses. My old ways of self-regulation and coping included so much cannabis, sex to numb myself out and retraumatize myself, and disordered eating. It was freeing when I finally learned there were actually healthy ways I could learn to regulate my body. Here are a couple different ways to self-regulate.

- **Mindful breathing.** I've heard people say that they don't like to do mindful breathing because it makes them feel even more anxious. Like the thought of having to hold your breath for a long time under water. Focusing on the breath does take some practice, but once you find something that works for you, it can make all the difference.

  I've found a breathing pattern of 4–7–7 that works great for me on those days or instances that I'm really struggling. I'm able to lean in to my breath in a pretty incredible way.

  Try this:

  Breathe in for a slow count of four.
  Hold the breath for a count of seven.
  Exhale for another slow count of seven.
  Repeat and notice after two to three minutes that your body is calming itself.

- **Sensory love.** Are you moved by a particular scene, song, natural spot, scent, or action like petting an animal? God has provided us with innumerable lovely things on this planet to tune into so that we tune out of some of the negative or overwhelming things we might be feeling. I am very soothed by waves on a body of water, so if I can't sit on a beach somewhere, then I sometimes play ocean sounds on an app. Try a new way to tickle the senses every day—this mindful action can be very healing.

- **Grounding.** This is an evidence-based strategy that helps you focus your attention and connect with your body and surroundings. For trauma survivors and people in recovery, this can help us to interrupt cycles of toxic thinking or intrusive thoughts and find calm. This might sound a bit fluffy and not super practical, so let's do a grounding exercise now.

  Notice where you are in the room. Are you sitting or standing? Are you lying down or reclined? Feel your feet on the floor, or feel the sensation of where your body touches the surface where you are seated or resting. What does it feel like?

  What does it look like in your space? Do you have pictures? Pets? A wild, painted accent wall? Do you have candles or books or screens around you? Keep noticing your surroundings and how your body feels in this moment right where you are. Now.

Resilience Practice #3: Name Your Feelings

Remember that it's okay to feel what you are feeling. A big part of my healing every day is allowing myself to feel certain things like anger, sadness, insecurity, and to name them. When we allow ourselves to feel, when we identify our feelings, something incredible happens: we can move on from them.

Try this:

> Get out your journal and write down what you are feeling. Name it. Then, if you feel comfortable and safe to do so, tell a trusted friend what you are feeling.

Resilience Practice #4: Connect in Community

Following a trauma, you may want to withdraw from others, but isolation can be harmful. I've experienced this firsthand. Allowing others into our experience can be scary—but such an important healing thing.

Let's chat a little bit more about how we can connect with others when it's tough.

- **Ask for help.** You may be like me and were raised in a way that made reaching out for help unsafe—or even impossible. It's no wonder that sometimes we think that we have to get through things on our own. Or that only we can help ourselves. This is simply not true. As human beings, we were made for connection.

    While we indeed need to seek help, it's also important to state that it's okay to be selective about who we share our experiences and vulnerabilities with. Some people are safe and some people are not. I'll say this again in a minute, but your story is your story. You get to choose who you share with, how you share, and who you reach out to for support and help.

There are so many resources out there today that offer support. Faith communities that feel safe and are equipped to support individuals in trauma recovery, counselors, physicians, treatment professionals, or recovery coaches are just a few examples of people and places that can be there for you if you reach out. You can read stories from other women on Circle of Chairs. You are not alone.

- **Own your story.** It's an empowering thing to be able to choose who to let into our lives and who to be vulnerable with. Your story is your story. Not everyone wants to talk about their experience on social media and that's okay. It's also important to consider that we don't have to *ever* go into the details of our trauma if we aren't ready. Connecting doesn't have to involve sharing explicit details of our stories or trauma.

  While you may want to share details, healing can come from the simple acts of learning to trust and letting others love and care about us and then moving into deeper places of healing and addressing trauma when we are ready and have the necessary supports in place.

  Here are some of my favorite ways to connect in the community:

  - Attend sober activities and events with a friend you trust.

- Check out social media accounts and other resources from people you respect and look up to in the recovery community.
- Attend support groups for trauma survivors and gender-specific meetings.
- Find ways to be of service and volunteer.

Resilience Practice #5: Take Care of Your Physical Health

Having a healthy body can help us to cope with the stress of everyday life and with trauma. Below are a couple of tried-and-true things that we can all prioritize that will help us get to a place of health and wellness. Many of these are simple—what we learned in middle school—yet sometimes even the simplest concepts can be tough. Especially when we aren't used to caring for ourselves.

So, what are some ways that we can prioritize our physical health?

- **Sleep hygiene.** Routine, baths, meditation, reading, and limiting screen time can all be helpful; naps are fun too!
- **Avoid alcohol and drugs.** Their use can worsen your trauma symptoms and increase feelings of depression, anxiety, and isolation.
- **Eat a well-balanced diet.** Eating small, balanced meals throughout the day will help you keep your energy up and minimize mood swings. Avoid sugary and fried foods and snack when you need to. If you find yourself not able to afford healthy food or you don't know what

to buy, there are great nutritionists out there. Contact me and we can work on finding more info for you in your area. Remember, too, this can be a tough area for women in recovery especially, and I know this first-hand from working through disordered eating in recovery and active addiction.

- **Reduce stress.** We talked about this when we talked about movement, but there are other relaxation techniques that you can try, like the breathing or grounding exercises above.

When I think about how I'm caring for my physical health, I like to think about how I would treat a hurting friend or beloved pet. Am I giving myself the same kind of gentle treatment, loving care, and opportunity for rest?

Keep Going

I hope these five resilience practices will help you to lean in to your struggle a bit more. When we lean in, instead of opting out, we are giving ourselves the loving opportunity to heal and disrupt those unhealthy patterns that keep us stuck.

I want to end by saying that there are times when it is helpful or even necessary to seek additional professional help for trauma. If you need more support, please get it. There are some wonderful resources at the Substance Abuse and Mental Health Services Administration (SAMHSA) treatment locator: www.samhsa.gov/find-help or 1-800-662-HELP.

Acknowledgments

The acknowledgments page of a book is somewhere I like to visit first when I pick up a new book. I like to sit with the author for a moment as they recognize and honor the process. I hope you will sit with me for a moment more to see all the people involved in making these pages and movements of healing come to life. If you are like me and reading this first: I see you.

Thank you first and foremost to my mother, Diana, who opens her heart and soul in these pages. Being vulnerable takes courage, trust, and ultimately hope that God will do something with the dirt and transform it. The vulnerability was painful at times for both of us: imagine laying it all out there (and by *all*, I mean some really tough experiences) for the world to see and hoping someone will gain something from it. It's tough. I'm so grateful for our relationship, Mom. I've also learned over time that, like the process of recovery (when we sit in a circle of chairs and share the innermost parts of our sordid lives), the healing can go both ways. I hope, Mom, that your showing up for the reader was also a journey of deeper healing for you too.

Thank you to my husband for your amazing support and belief in me, and to my kids for being their amazing little selves. My hope is that you will both live lives of healing and grace and be able to share this with the next generation.

Next, I'd like to thank the people who live in these pages: David Morris with Lake Drive Books, who helped a series of rhythms emerge and had patience for the message to develop. Thank you for asking tough questions, believing that authors like me deserve the expert guidance and the trust that you have graciously shown. Andy Rogers, your insight and gentle guidance not only made this book better but helped me grow as a writer one comment and red line at a time. Mike and Amy Salisbury, for your continued encouragement, consultation, and publishing expertise, along with the folks at Yates and Yates for starting the Author Coaching Program. In a changing publishing landscape, you all are leading the way to help good books with a purpose get into the hands of readers who need them. For my writing community at the Grit and Grace Project, especially Darlene Brock, Ashley Johnson, Tess Lopez, and Allison McCormick. I can't thank you enough for the encouragement, support, and community. My books would not be here if you hadn't have said, "Yes, welcome." My church family, including the mom's small group and First Recovery, thank you for reminding me of what is truly important and for the opportunity to stay grounded in the local community: Katie, Katie, Lauren, and Sara. Kristi Younkin for being my partner in Circle of Chairs and for your gentle and bold wisdom. Melinda Holder for your uncanny ability to get me to share my dirt and for being a true sister. Dr. Dawn Nickels, Lisa, Carrie, Suzie, and Sara: you continue to inspire me and encourage me to stay on mission. Flo, Elliot, Emily, Shelly, Carolyn, Denna, and all of the people unnamed here who have helped to make a way in the wilderness.

And last but not least, I thank God that I have been entrusted with this calling. May I always put you first. May you always have the last word.

Endnotes

Introduction
1. Brennan Manning, *The Wisdom of Tenderness: What Happens When God's Fierce Mercy Transforms Our Lives* (San Francisco: HarperOne, 2004).
2. Russell Stafford, "Specimen Trees and Shrubs with Elegantly Twisted Branches," Fafard.com, accessed March 13, 2024.
3. Bessel van der Kolk, "How the Body Keeps the Score on Trauma," Big Think, YouTube, November 22, 2024.
4. Trey Ferguson, *Theologizin' Bigger: Homilies on Living Freely and Loving Wholly* (Grand Rapids: Lake Drive Books, 2024).
5. Joan Walsh Anglund, *A Cup of Sun: A Book of Poems* (Boston: Houghton Mifflin Harcourt, 1967).
6. Alcoholics Anonymous World Services, *The Official "Big Book" from Alcoholics Anonymous, Fourth Edition* (New York: Alcoholics Anonymous World Services, 2023).

Chapter 1
7. Bonnie S. Dansky, Michael E. Saladin, Kathleen T. Brady, Dean G. Kilpatrick, and Heidi S. Resnick, "Prevalence of Victimization and Posttraumatic Stress Disorder among Women with Substance Use Disorders: Comparison of Telephone and In-Person Assessment Samples," *International Journal of Mental Health and Addiction* 30, no. 9 (July 1995): 1079–99, https://doi.org/10.3109/10826089509055829.
8. Pamela J. Brown, Robert L. Stout, and Jolyne Gannon-Rowley, "Substance Use Disorder-PTSD Comorbidity: Patients' Perceptions of Symptom Interplay and Treatment Issues," *Journal of Substance Abuse Treatment* 15, no. 5 (1998): 445–448, https://doi.org/10.1016/s0740-5472(97)00286-9.
9. Bessel van der Kolk, *The Body Keeps the Score: Brain, Mind, and Body in the Healing of Trauma* (New York: Penguin Books, 2014), 206.
10. Nora M. Al Aboud, Connor Tupper, and Ishwarlal Jialal, "Genetics, Epigenetic Mechanism," StatPearls (January 2023), https://www.ncbi.nlm.nih.gov/books/NBK532999/.

Chapter 2
11. Cheryl Strayed, *Wild: From Lost to Found on the Pacific Crest Trail* (New York: Knopf, 2012).
12. Anne Frank, *The Diary of a Young Girl* (New York: Bantam, 1993).

13. Claire Gillespie, "What Is Generational Trauma?" Health.com, updated August 11, 2023, https://www.health.com/condition/ptsd/generational-trauma.
14. John J. Sigal, Vincenzo F. Dinicola, and Michael Buonvino, "Grandchildren of Survivors: Can Negative Effects of Prolonged Exposure to Excessive Stress be Observed Two Generations Later?" *The Canadian Journal of Psychiatry* 33, no. 3 (1988): 207–212, https://doi.org/10.1177/070674378803300309.
15. Gillespie, "What Is Generational Trauma?"

Chapter 3
16. W. Lee Warren, *Hope Is the First Dose: A Treatment Plan for Recovering from Trauma, Tragedy, and Other Massive Things* (Colorado Springs: WaterBrook & Multnomah, 2023).
17. Nona Jones, "Nona Jones Ministries | Meet Nona," accessed October 29, 2023, https://www.nonajones.com/meet-nona.

Chapter 4
18. Brené Brown, *The Gifts of Imperfection: Let Go of Who You Think You're Supposed to Be and Embrace Who You Are* (Center City: Hazelden Publishing, 2010).
19. Ida Soghomonian, "Boundaries—Why Are They Important? Part 1," The Resilience Centre, September 23, 2019, https://www.theresiliencecentre.com.au/boundaries-why-are-they-important/.
20. Mayo Clinic Staff, "Being Assertive: Reduce Stress, Communicate Better," Mayo Clinic, January 20, 2024, https://www.mayoclinic.org/healthy-lifestyle/stress-management/in-depth/assertive/art-20044644.

Chapter 5
21. van der Kolk, *The Body Keeps the Score.*
22. Centers for Disease Control and Prevention, "Fast Facts: Preventing Adverse Childhood Experiences," CDC.gov, updated June 29, 2023, https://www.cdc.gov/aces/about/.
23. CDC, "Fast Facts: Preventing Adverse Childhood Experiences."

Chapter 6
24. Philip Yancey, *Soul Survivor: How Thirteen Unlikely Mentors Helped My Faith Survive the Church* (Colorado Springs: Waterbrook, 2003), 7.
25. Philip Yancey, *Disappointment with God: Three Questions No One Asks Aloud* (Grand Rapids: Zondervan, 1988), 49.
26. "Dr. Paul Wilson Brand," International Leprosy Association—History of Leprosy, updated September 15, 2006, https://leprosyhistory.org/database/person31.
27. Yancey, *Soul Survivor.*
28. Heather Harpham Kopp, *Sober Mercies: How Love Caught Up with a Christian Drunk* (Nashville: Jericho Books, 2013).
29. Manda Carpenter, *Soul Care to Save Your Life* (Ada: Baker Books, 2022).
30. Centers for Disease Control and Prevention, "Risk and Protective Factors," CDC.gov, updated June 29, 2023, https://www.cdc.gov/aces/risk-factors/index.html.

Chapter 7

31. Caroline Beidler, "This Is What I Would Say to the Man Who Raped Me," *Grit and Grace Life*, accessed October 29, 2023, https://thegritandgraceproject.org/herstory/this-is-what-i-would-say-to-the-man-who-raped-me.

32. Manda Carpenter and Stephanie Duncan Smith, "125: What Will Make Me a Better Writer?" April 19, 2023, in *A Longer Table*, podcast, https://podcasters.spotify.com/pod/show/a-longer-table/episodes/125-What-Will-Make-Me-A-Better-Writer-e22jldn/a-a9mifap.

33. Anne Lamott, *Bird by Bird: Some Instructions on Writing and Life* (New York: Anchor Books, 1994).

34. Corrie ten Boom, "Guideposts Classics: Corrie ten Boom on Forgiveness," originally titled "I'm Still Learning to Forgive," *Guideposts*, November 1972.

35. Corrie ten Boom, "I'm Still Learning to Forgive."

36. Kate Baer, *What Kind of Woman: Poems* (New York: Harper Perennial, 2020).

Chapter 8

37. Texas Master Gardener, "Insect Metamorphosis," Galveston County Master Gardeners: Texas A&M AgriLife Extension Service, accessed March 29, 2024, https://txmg.org/galveston/beneficials-in-the-garden-and-landscape/insect-metamorphosis/.

38. Sheryl Sandberg, *Lean In: Women, Work, and the Will to Lead* (New York: Knopf, 2013).

39. Candace Osmond, "What Does 'Lean In' Mean?" Grammarist, May 3, 2016, https://grammarist.com/phrase/lean-in/.

40. Lisa M. Najavits, *Seeking Safety: A Treatment Manual for PTSD and Substance Abuse*, Treatment Innovations, 2019, https://www.treatment-innovations.org/seeking-safety.html.

41. Najavits, *Seeking Safety.* https://www.treatment-innovations.org/seeking-safety.html.

42. Sonya Norman, Jessica Hamblen, and Paula P. Schnurr, "Overview of Psychotherapy for PTSD," U.S. Department of Veterans Affairs: National Center for PTSD, accessed October 2023, https://www.ptsd.va.gov/professional/treat/txessentials/overview_therapy.asp.

43. "The Neurobiology of Attachment and How that Profoundly Impacts the Treatment of Trauma," National Institute for the Clinical Application of Behavioral Medicine, accessed 2024, https://www.nicabm.com/program/attachment/.

44. "PTSD Treatments," in the *Clinical Practice Guideline for the Treatment of Posttraumatic Stress Disorder*, American Psychological Association, last updated June 2020, https://www.apa.org/ptsd-guideline/treatments.

45. Patrick Hendry, "CPS Blog: Trauma-Informed Peer Support," Mental Health America, accessed 2024, https://mhanational.org/cps-blog-trauma-informed-peer-support.

Chapter 9

46. Caroline Beidler, "'What about the Men? . . .'" *Circle of Chairs*, February 27, 2024, https://carolinebeidler.substack.com/p/what-about-the-men.

47. "Root Diseases," Forest Pathology, accessed 2024, https://forestpathology.org/root-diseases/.

48. Kim Mellen-McLean, Bruce G. Marcot, Janet L. Ohmann, Karen Waddell, Elizabeth A. Willhite, Steven A. Acker, Susan A. Livingston, Bruce B. Hostetler, Barbara S. Webb, and Barbara A. Garcia, "Black Stain Root Disease: *Grosmannia wageneri*," DecAID, accessed March 13, 2024, https://apps.fs.usda.gov/r6_decaid/views/black_stain_root_disease.html#important_habitats.

49. Rachel Marie Kang, *The Matter of Little Losses: Finding Grace to Grieve the Big (and Small) Things* (Ada: Baker Books, 2024).

50. The Editors of Encyclopædia Britannica, "Root," *Encyclopedia Britannica,* updated March 19, 2024, https://www.britannica.com/science/root-plant.

51. Kyaien O. Conner, "Why Historical Trauma Is Critical to Understanding Black Mental Health," *Psychology Today*, October 1, 2020.

Chapter 10

52. "Home," Joel Freeman Fitness, accessed November 1, 2023, https://www.joelfreemanfitness.com.

53. Tiffany Ayuda, "What Really Happens to Your Body When You Lift Weights Every Day," LIVESTRONG.COM, updated September 8, 2020, https://www.livestrong.com/article/151501-the-effects-of-lifting-weights-everyday.

54. Glennon Doyle, *Untamed* (New York: The Dial Press, 2020).

55. Dallas Willard, "Spiritual Formation: What It Is, and How It Is Done," dwillard.org, accessed March 30, 2024, https://www.christianitytoday.com/biblestudies/articles/spiritualformation/beingformed.

56. Caroline Beidler, "5 Everyday Spiritual Practices to Grow Your Faith," *Grit and Grace Life*, accessed November 1, 2023, https://thegritandgraceproject.org/faith/5-everyday-spiritual-practices-to-grow-your-faith.

57. John Throop, "5 Facets in Spiritual Formation," *Christianity Today*, May 24, 2011, https://www.christianitytoday.com/biblestudies/articles/spiritualformation/beingformed.

58. Madeleine L'Engle, *Walking on Water: Reflections on Faith and Art* (Chicago: Harold Shaw Publishers, 1980).

59. Eugene H. Peterson, *A Long Obedience in the Same Direction: Discipleship in an Instant Society* (Lisle, Illinois: IVP Books, 2000).

60. Laura McKowen, *We Are the Luckiest: The Surprising Magic of a Sober Life* (Novato, California: New World Library, 2020).

61. Throop, "5 Facets in Spiritual Formation."

Chapter 11

62. Heather Harpham Kopp, *Sober Mercies: How Love Caught Up with a Christian Drunk* (Nashville: Jericho Books, 2013).

63. Kopp, *Sober Mercies.*

Chapter 12

64. Langston Hughes, "Fulfillment."

65. Brown, *The Gifts of Imperfection*, 70.

66. Cole Arthur Riley, *This Here Flesh: Spirituality, Liberation, and the Stories That Make Us* (New York: Convergent Books, 2022), 39.

67. Ann Patchett, *This Is the Story of a Happy Marriage* (New York: HarperCollins, 2013).

68. Leslie Bennetts, "The Unsinkable Jennifer Aniston," *Vanity Fair*, October 10, 2006.

Chapter 13

69. "Trauma," American Psychological Association, n.d., accessed April 1, 2024, https://www.apa.org/topics/trauma.

70. Henri J. M. Nouwen, *Turn My Mourning into Dancing: Finding Hope in Hard Times* (Nashville: Thomas Nelson, 2004).

Chapter 14

71. Max Lucado, "Grace: More Than We Deserve, Greater Than We Imagine," interview by *Christianity Today*, May 7, 2013, https://www.christianitytoday.com/bible-studies/articles/spiritualformation/grace-more-than-we-deserve-greater-than-we-imagine.html.

72. Philip Yancey, *Reaching for the Invisible God* (Grand Rapids: Zondervan, 2002).

73. Chuck Swindoll, "Book of James Overview—Insight for Living Ministries." Insight.org, 2020, https://insight.org/resources/bible/the-general-epistles/james.

74. Carpenter, *Soul Care to Save Your Life*, 20.

75. "Cheryl Strayed Interview," accessed April 22, 2024, www.youtube.com/watch?v=Ws3AXmrDQvI.

76. Maggie Smith, *You Could Make This Place Beautiful: A Memoir* (New York, NY: Atria/One Signal Publishers, 2023).

77. *The Anonymous People*, directed by Greg Williams (New York: Kino Lorber, 2013).

78. "Circle of Chairs: Storytelling with a Purpose," Circle of Chairs, accessed November 1, 2023, https://www.circleofchairs.com/.

Chapter 15

79. Dani Shapiro, *Hourglass: Time, Memory, Marriage* (New York: Knopf, 2017).

80. Kathleen Brown-Rice, "Examining the Theory of Historical Trauma among Native Americans," *The Professional Counselor* 3, no. 3 (2013): 117–130.

81. Smith, M.D. (2019). "Counting the Dead: Estimating the Loss of Life in the Indigenous Holocaust, 1492-Present," Accessed April, 21, 2024 from https://www.se.edu/native-american/wp-content/uploads/sites/49/2019/09/A-NAS-2017-Proceedings-Smith.pdf.

82. "Tips for Disaster Responders: Understanding Historical Trauma and Resilience When Responding to an Event in Indian Country," SAMHSA, publication ID: PEP22-01-01-005, October 2022.

83. Brown-Rice, "Examining the Theory of Historical Trauma among Native Americans."

84. Brown-Rice, "Examining the Theory of Historical Trauma among Native Americans."

85. "What Is Epigenetics?" Centers for Disease Control and Prevention, last reviewed August 15, 2022.

86. Center on the Developing Child, "What Is Epigenetics?" infographic, Harvard University, accessed 2019.

87. Conner, "Why Historical Trauma Is Critical to Understanding Black Mental Health."

88. Anita Phillips and Jennie Allen, "The Emotional Impact of 2020 with Dr. Anita Phillips," *Made for This with Jennie Allen* podcast, September 1, 2020.

Chapter 16

89. John Mark McMillan, "Song Story: How He Loves," interview by Editorial Team, *Worship Leader*, January 4, 2016.
90. C. S. Lewis, *Surprised by Joy: The Shape of My Early Life* (London: Harcourt Brace Jovanovich, 1955).
91. Riley, *This Here Flesh*.

Chapter 17

92. Yancey, *Disappointment with God*.

Conclusion

93. Beronda Montgomery, "Trees Don't Rush to Heal from Trauma and Neither Should We," *Psyche*, February 1, 2022.
94. E. O., "A New Freedom and a New Happiness," *AAGrapevine*, July 1985, accessed December 8, 2023.
95. Riley, *This Here Flesh*.

About the Author

Caroline Beidler, BA, MSW is an author, recovery advocate, and founder of the storytelling platform Circle of Chairs. She is also the author of *Downstairs Church: Finding Hope in the Grit of Addiction and Trauma Recovery*. With almost twenty years in leadership within social work and ministry, she is currently a consultant with JBS International, writing and creating content for federal agencies like the Office of Recovery and the Substance Abuse and Mental Health Services Administration, and a correspondent with *Recovery Today Magazine*. She is also the founder and host of the annual International Women's Day Global Recovery Event. Caroline lives in Tennessee with her husband and twins where she enjoys hiking in the mountains and building up her community's local recovery ministry.

Diana Dalles, LPN, MSSW has been writing poetry and journaling since her teenage years, mainly for her own enjoyment and healing. She spent the early years of her career in the nursing field, then worked thirty-five years as a professional social worker. Her employment interests included hospice, medical social work, and gerontology. She has facilitated grief, trauma, and women's empowerment groups. Diana retired in 2015, and being with her family brings her the greatest joy. She also gardens for herself and others, and stays active in nature. She volunteers at a local food pantry and is involved in her church's ministries. Diana lives with her cat in a small rural Wisconsin town.

Join Caroline's newsletter, *Circle of Chairs*, on Substack here:

About Lake Drive Books

Lake Drive Books is an independent publishing company offering books that help you heal, grow, and discover. We champion books about values and strategies, not ideologies, and authors who are spiritually rich, contextually intelligent, and focused on human flourishing. We want to help readers feel seen.

If you like this or any of our other books at lakedrivebooks. com, we could use your help: please follow our authors on social media, subscribe to their newsletters, and tell others what you think of their remarkable books.

Printed in the USA
CPSIA information can be obtained
at www.ICGtesting.com
LVHW040317140824
788071LV00003B/17